PREPARE THE WAY

AN ADVENT DEVOTIONAL

SUSANNAH BAKER

VISTA OAKS

Find me on my website at susannahbaker.com.

First paperback edition November 2024
Published by Vista Oaks
SusannahBaker.com

Cover and book design by Daly Rea

All Scripture quotations are taken from the ESV® Bible (The Holy Bible, English Standard Version®), copyright © 2001 by Crossway, a publishing ministry of Good News Publishers. Used by permission. All rights reserved.

Printed in the United States of America
ISBN: 9798343454130

A voice cries:
"In the wilderness PREPARE THE WAY of the Lord;
make straight in the desert a highway for our God.
Every valley shall be lifted up,
and every mountain and hill be made low;
the uneven ground shall become level,
and the rough places a plain.
And the glory of the Lord shall be revealed,
and all flesh shall see it together,
for the mouth of the Lord has spoken."

Isaiah 40:3-5

To Gregg and Kelly Matte
whose Mondays look like their Sundays

~

Thank you for faithfully preparing the way
for the coming King.

CONTENTS

PREPARE THE WAY

The word "Advent" brings up as many different definitions as there are people who celebrate Christmas. But Advent is derived from the Latin word *adventus*, meaning "coming."[1] Advent is a season of preparation for the coming King. But so often in the rush of preparing for Christmas, we forget to prepare for the King. Our stockings are full, but our hearts are empty and weary. This is why I felt a tug years ago to write these devotionals. It was a reminder to me, as much as to anyone, to stop, listen, and enter into the divine majesty and mystery of the days leading up to Christmas.

Through the years, I have learned Advent is as much about looking forward as it is about looking back. When I first wrote a series of Advent devotionals twenty years ago, my focus was on the past and the first time Christ came. But now that I am older and have endured more suffering, I have become more dissatisfied with what this world has to offer. As more people I know and love now wait for me in heaven, my focus has shifted even more to the future. Christmas is as much about looking ahead to the King who is coming again as it about remembering the King who came.

As Jonathon Gibson so beautifully writes in his Advent liturgy book *O Come, O Come, Emmanuel*, "the [Advent] season is not about what we can do for Christ by our work or prayers or fasting; rather, it is about what he has done for us in *his* work and prayers and fasting—a work that began in his first coming in humility and which will conclude in his second coming in glory."[2]

This Christmas, you and I stand between the two advents of Christ. I am inviting you on a journey to prepare the way for the King together. We are to marvel in gratitude and awe at the humility of His manger and meditate with hope and longing at the certainty of His return.

To help us do this, I have provided a devotional for each day of the Advent season, with the following elements:

- A Scripture to READ
- A devotional to PREPARE your heart
- Three questions to CONSIDER
- A prayer to PRAY

The devotionals for the four Sundays of Advent as well as for Christmas Day also include Advent Activities for the week as well as a Closing Carol to sing.

As we enjoy Advent together over the next four weeks, remember that no matter how many items are still on your to-do list or how you sound as you sing the Christmas carols, what matters is the One who came. For the road to Bethlehem was the road to Calvary, and the same road reminds us Christ will come again. So prepare the way during this Advent Season—prepare the way for the coming of your King.

With you in the journey,

PREPARING AN
ADVENT WREATH

Advent always begins the fourth Sunday before Christmas and goes through Christmas Eve. The number of days can vary each year depending on how many days are between the fourth Sunday of Advent and Christmas Day. But no matter the length of Advent each year, you will always have four full weeks of devotions to use in this book, as well as one for Christmas Day. If you're using these devotionals in a year when Advent is shorter than the full four weeks, you can skip a few devotions the last week or use them for the days following Christmas.

To add to the symbolism and festivity of Advent, some people assemble a wreath made with evergreens (real or artificial) and five candles. Four of the candles are placed evenly around the wreath, and the fifth is placed in the wreath's center. The color of the candles varies according to tradition, but typically three of the four candles in the wreath are purple (the color of royalty) and the fourth candle is pink (the color of joy). The candle in the center is usually white and is called the Christ candle. During each Sunday of Advent, an additional candle is lit until the last Sunday before Christmas, all four candles are burning. Christmas Day, all five candles are lit, the candle in the center representing the coming of the Christ child into a dark and dreary world.

For the four weeks of Advent, I have chosen Scripture readings and written devotionals to correspond with the traditional Advent themes: the Prophet's candle and hope; the Bethlehem candle and peace; the Shepherd's candle and joy; and the Angel's candle and love.

My hope for each of us throughout this season is that we find quiet moments filled with beauty and joy to commemorate, welcome, anticipate, and prepare for the coming King.

ADVENT
WEEK ONE

THE PROPHET'S CANDLE: HOPE

THE FIRST SUNDAY OF ADVENT
Come, Thou Long Expected Jesus

Before you begin reading, light the first candle on your wreath, the Prophet's Candle, which represents hope.

READ

Genesis 2:15-18; 3:1-15

PREPARE

My attempts at gardening have not been very promising. In fact, I seem to kill more than I nurture and grow. It's not that I don't try; I really do. I water, fertilize, prune, watch, and wait. But my flowers don't often flourish under my care. Still, my garden brings me joy and delight. I love to walk through it in the cool of the day, looking over the plants, pulling the weeds, and soaking in the smells. A peaceful calm surrounds me every time I step into the yard.

Most gardens are peaceful places, havens from the hustle and bustle of daily life. Their rhythms and cycles of growth are a respite from the frantic pace of urban life, reminding us there is a time for every season: a time for planting, pruning, dying, waiting, and blooming once again. But the real reason I like gardens so much is that life and relationship with God began in a garden. God could have placed Adam and Eve anywhere in creation, but He chose a garden, where He walked and talked with them.

Gardens remind us that although winter comes every year and leaves fall off the trees leaving the branches bare, the promise of spring always remains. Hope runs strong in the veins of a winter garden, for somehow it knows winter will not last forever. Winter is only a season. So, it is with those who follow Christ. Although disobedience and sin first occurred in the garden, it is also the place where hope was introduced. Embedded in the words of the curse are God's words of promise to undo the curse of sin and return us to the goodness of garden-like intimacy with Him (Genesis 3:15).

The first candle we light, the Prophet's Candle, stands for the hope passed down through generations from the time of Adam to the time of Christ. The curse of death and eternal separation from God entered the world with sin. But even in the garden of Eden God prophesied that One would come from the seed of a woman who would crush the serpent's head. Through the centuries, God sent prophets—His messengers to a dark and dying world—to remind His people that a Savior would come to redeem all of creation and to make all things new.

So, we wait with high hopes during Advent. Although the Messiah has come, we still eagerly wait for Him to come again. Beneath the surface of our excitement for the Christmas season is an ache for our true home. We are still waiting for justice and peace to rule the earth and for face-to-face intimacy with God to be fully restored. But we do not wait in vain. We wait in hope just like the prophets of old who waited for the Messiah, believing God would faithfully fulfill the promises of His Word. Our hope rests in the day when the clouds will part, the trumpet will sound, and those who know Jesus will go to be with Him in our forever home. As the angels proclaim: hope has come, and hope will return, fulfilling our longing to return to the garden.

CONSIDER

- When have you had to wait a long time for something you wanted to occur?

- What did you do during that season to keep your heart from becoming anxious, cynical, or afraid?

- During the season of Advent, how can you wait with a heart that is expectant for Jesus's coming instead of distracted by the activity that so quickly consumes us?

ADVENT ACTIVITIES

Choose one of the following activities this week to help you remember what waiting and hoping are all about during this season.

- **Make cookies.** As you wait for the cookies to finish baking, consider other things that are tough to wait for. Consider how hard it was for God's people to wait for Jesus's first coming—and how tough it can sometimes be for us to wait for His return. Think about how you can include your family and/or friends in this activity.

    If you have kids, explain that while waiting for cookies

to bake is hard, waiting for thousands of years for Jesus to come to earth was even harder. As you taste the cookies when they come out of the oven, explain how the sweetness of the cookies is only a small part of the sweetness Jesus brought when He came.

- **Create a prayer chain.** Cut out strips of red and green construction paper, one strip for each of the days before Christmas. On each strip of paper, write the name of family member, friend, or person who is going through a hard time or who does not know Jesus. Alternate the red and green strips of paper and tape the ends together to form a paper chain. Hang the chain on your Christmas tree.

  Each day before Christmas, tear off a link. Each time you tear off a link, stop and pray for the person whose name is on the ring. Consider how prayer is the best way we can have hope for others who are hurting or who do not know the Lord.

  If you have teens or kids who are old enough to write, allow them to write their own prayer requests on a few of the chain links. If you have younger kids, invite them to call out a few names and ideas to you as you write them on the slips of paper. Allow them to take turns removing the chains from the link each day as well.

PRAY

Father,

Thank You for sending Your Son to be the Savior of the world as You promised through the prophets. Remind us during Advent to focus on the coming of Christ rather than on the constant activity and commotion that surrounds us. May You find us to be a people ready for Your return, for You are the hope of every heart. Amen.

CLOSING CAROL:
"COME, THOU LONG-EXPECTED JESUS"

Come, thou long-expected Jesus,
born to set thy people free;
from our fears and sins release us,
let us find our rest in thee.
Israel's strength and consolation,
hope of all the earth thou art;
dear desire of every nation,
joy of every longing heart.

Born thy people to deliver,
born a child, and yet a King,
born to reign in us forever,
now thy gracious kingdom bring.
By thine own eternal Spirit
rule in all our hearts alone;
by thine all sufficient merit
raise us to thy glorious throne.

MONDAY
Jacob's Star

READ

Numbers 24:15-19

PREPARE

To understand the essence of Advent, we have to look at some of creation's first groanings for a Savior. As we saw, prophecies of the Messiah came as early as the garden of Eden, and they continued through the first five books of the Bible. Numbers, the fourth book of the Bible is a story of desert wandering. Because the generation of Israelites God delivered out of Egypt refused to believe He was strong enough and good enough to deliver them safely to the promised land, they were forced to wander for forty years in a dry and barren part of the wilderness, fully dependent on God for protection, direction, and daily sustenance.

Many of us have spent our days as desert wanderers. While dwelling in the land of promise—a place of peace, rest, intimacy, and dependence on Christ—is possible, we instead choose the unrest of independence, fear, and unbelief in the character and promises of God. No matter what, we stubbornly cling to our independence, refusing to give up our wandering ways and make our home in the sheltering presence of God.

Yet in a rebellious generation of people whose hearts had wandered far from God, a prophet saw a star.

For a desert dweller, the function of a star is simple: it gives direction, permanence, and stability in an ever-changing landscape. God's promise of a star that will rise from His people shows every wandering heart the possibility of finding the way back to Him.

No matter how wayward our steps become, how temporary our homes on this earth may be, or how often circumstances and seasons change, the promise of the permanence, stability, and beauty of Jacob's star rises over our hearts again and again. It is not a prize we earn for being so steadfast or good; it is a gift of grace we receive because we have a good heavenly Father who still goes after all who are lost and wandering.

Jesus says in His final word to the church in Revelation: "I am the root and the descendant of David, the bright morning star" (Revelation 22:16). Jesus doesn't simply tell us the way to the land of promise, peace, and rest, He *is* the way. While many of our steps may feel purposeless in the here and now, "God writes straight with crooked lines."[3] For everyone who calls on His name and hopes in His promises, God redeems their wayward hearts and brings them to a secure and permanent home through relationship with Jesus.

We will always have the tendency to wander, just like the Israelites. But as we follow Christ and look up and out to the rising of the bright morning star, our journey becomes less of an aimless pilgrimage and more of a journey that leads us home. So, look up from the desert this Advent season and follow Jacob's Star.

CONSIDER

- When have you been in a season of desert wandering? What was it like?

- How can the character and promises of God secure your heart when your circumstances and seasons change?

- What is one practical way you can depend on God to meet your needs and look up and out to Jesus instead of trying to figure out life on your own?

PRAY

Father,

Many of our days are still spent in wandering, even though You have given us Your Spirit and Word to lead us along safe and secure paths (Psalm 23:3). When things feel unstable around us, lift our gaze to Jesus and fix our eyes on the glorious light of Your Son. Lead us out of the desert of our disobedience and into the place of repentance, rest, trust, and peace. Amen.

TUESDAY
God with Us

READ

Isaiah 7:10-17

PREPARE

For many of us, this year may have been a year of loss—of dreams, hopes, employment, or even a beloved family member. The one word that truly brings comfort in this passage from the prophet Isaiah reminds us of all that we have gained: Immanuel. This is a much-needed reminder during the Advent season. For as exciting as Christmas is, the holidays can also be a painful reminder of what we are missing.

No matter how joyful the Christmas season is, we are all aware of an ache that runs beneath it. Living life here on this earth is like riding a broken bike. At some point, we all fall off, and we all emerge at the end of the year with skinned knees, broken bones, and hurting hearts.

To ignore the ache is to ignore the reason Jesus came. He did not come to make perfect people happy; He came to bring hurting people comfort and to make broken people whole.

This is why the promise of the prophet Isaiah wraps around us like a warm blanket as Christmas draws near. In all of our losses, we have this reminder that we have been our Immanuel, "God with us." His coming undoes the lie of evil that has echoed in our ears since the garden—the lie that says,

"You are unseen and unknown. You are helpless and can't even cry out for help. You are on your own."

Isaiah's words expose the lie of the evil one for what it is: baseless and untrue. God not only sees you this Advent season, but He also hears the cries of your heart—even the unspoken ones. He actively moves toward you as the God who is with you and for you in the form of Immanuel, His precious Son.

He is with the barren, the widowed, and the grieving. He is with the hurting, the longing, and the lonely. He answers the cry of the womb and the cry of every heart for help, for purpose, for a new identity, for a fresh start, for a family, and for a new name: "If God is for us, who can be against us? He who did not spare his own Son but gave him up for us all, how will he not also with him graciously give us all things?" (Romans 8:31-32).

If Advent is a lonely or painful time for you and your family, think on the Jesus, our Immanuel, and know that He comes to fill every empty space.

CONSIDER

- What things do you have to be thankful for this Christmas season?

- What losses are you mourning this Christmas season? How does the coming of Immanuel bring comfort and hope in your grief?

- Close your eyes and see Jesus coming for you today as Immanuel, God with you. Ask Him to make His presence known in tangible ways to you today.

PRAY

Father,

When You chose to create the world, You chose to send Your Son, for You knew Adam's race would need a Savior long before Jesus walked this earth. Thank You for sending us Immanuel, God with us. May we see Him moving toward us, healing our hurts, and comforting our hearts this Christmas season. Amen.

WEDNESDAY
The Coming of the King

READ

Isaiah 9:1-7

PREPARE

In J.R.R. Tolkien's classic *The Lord of the Rings*, a great shadow from the evil land of Mordor is attempting to sweep across all lands and peoples, but a great light dawns when the long-awaited king returns to rule his people. One of the prophecies about this king is "Life to the dying / In the king's hand lying!"[4] Toward the end of the book, the shadow is defeated, and the king goes to the wounded, healing those who have fallen under the darkness and sickness of the shadow, making his people whole again.

Through the curse of sin, the great shadow of death had fallen over the people of God. But in Isaiah's prophecy, a great light dawned with the coming of a King, "to us a child is born, to us a son is given" (Isaiah 9:6). After only a faint flicker of hope through the preceding ages, the coming of Christ now roared to life through Isaiah 9. Not only would the light of this King bring wisdom and healing, but it would also shatter every external yoke of bondage and break every internal bar of sin and oppression. The governing of the nations would forever rest on the shoulders of a King who is wonderful in counsel, mighty in power, everlasting in goodness, and peaceful in His rule and reign. While we see glimmers of the light of this King in the here and now, we still wait with great hope and longing for the full dawning of the light of His kingdom to be established on the earth. Our daily struggle is to not become engulfed in the despair of the shadow that still lingers but to live in confident hope that the fullness of His light will come.

In a letter to his fiancée, on December 13, 1943, Dietrich Bonhoeffer wrote from a Nazi German prison cell, "And then, just when everything is bearing down on us to such an extent that we can scarcely withstand it, the Christmas message comes to tell us that all our ideas are wrong, and that what we take to be evil and dark is really good and light because it come from God. Our eyes are at fault, that is all. God is in the manger, wealth in poverty, light in darkness, succor in abandonment. No evil can befall us; whatever men may do to us, they cannot but serve the God who is secretly revealed as love and rules the world and our lives."[5]

Just as Bonhoeffer did, as you see headlines of news of war, death, strife, and shadow, read between the lines. Soon the shadows will be gone, and we will walk in the light of the wisdom, truth, and love our perfect Ruler will bring. Jesus came once to the small village of Bethlehem, but He is coming again to rule and reign over all nations and over every heart.

CONSIDER

- When you read the news, what events most often trouble and worry you?

- What name of the child who was born and given to us speaks comfort and peace to your heart today (Isaiah 9:6)?

- How will the kingdom of Christ bring ultimate healing to every heart and nation when He comes again?

PRAY

Father,

Thank You for sending Jesus, our Wonderful Counselor, Mighty God, Everlasting Father, and Prince of Peace. When the shadows of darkness, suffering, and sin threaten to overwhelm us, help us to remember our great and glorious King is coming again. No matter what the headlines in the news tell us, give us the courage to live in His kingdom of light, opposing the darkness that threatens to overwhelm us, waiting in hope for His return. Amen.

THURSDAY
The Humble King

READ

Zechariah 9:9-17

PREPARE

Celebrities are usually thought of as unapproachable and untouchable. They are protected by bodyguards and live behind double-bolted doors. But if they ever come into town, you know about it. Their arrivals are trumpeted by news headlines, limousines, and private jets.

But as Zechariah prophesied, when the King of kings and the Lord of lords made His celebrated entrance into Jerusalem, He was not unapproachable, riding behind the wheels of a gilded chariot flanked by a legion of Roman guards. He was humble, riding a donkey, flanked by His disciples (Zechariah 9:9).

I think this is why we often miss Christ in the Christmas season. We set the stage for Him to come in the middle of extravagant gifts, expensive parties, and elaborate decorations. But we forget this is not how He came or where we find Him. In the Sermon on the Mount, Jesus said, "Blessed are the poor in spirit, for theirs is the kingdom of heaven. Blessed are those who mourn, for they shall be comforted" (Matthew 5:3-4). Jesus was not extolling poverty in and of itself: being poor is not synonymous with being blessed, but having poverty of spirit is. We must remember that in the middle of an extravagant season, we serve a gentle and humble Savior.

To prepare the way for Immanuel and see Jesus this Christmas season, we must do as Jesus did: "Have this mind among yourselves, which is yours in Christ Jesus, who, though he was in the form of God, did not count equality with God a thing to be grasped, but emptied himself, by taking the form of a servant, being born in the likeness of men. And being found in human form, he humbled himself by becoming obedient to the point of death, even death on a cross" (Philippians 2:5-8).

More than we want our homes, celebrations, and gifts to be perfect, we must want our hearts to be humble. Giving an expensive gift is easy; giving forgiveness is hard. Holding a party is simple; holding our tongues can feel impossible. Becoming irritable is effortless, but humbling ourselves and being generous with our time, attention, and grace requires spending ample time at the feet of our humble God.

Don't sacrifice humility for extravagance or perfection this Christmas season. And don't buy into the lie that the unapproachable people are the powerful people. There are no locked doors with Christ; He hides behind nothing and no one. He is always available, always vulnerable, always humble, and always reachable. "He never spends one hour without stooping to do the most menial work of cleansing filthy souls. And it is because of this humility He sits on the Throne and wields the scepter over hearts and worlds."[6] Come, let us adore our humble King.

CONSIDER

- How does reflecting on Jesus's humility take the pressure off you to have a perfect or extravagant Christmas this year?

- What is one way you can give the gift of a kind and attentive presence to your family or friends this Christmas season?

- What are practical ways you can have a humble heart this Christmas season? Who do you need to forgive or give grace?

PRAY

Father,

Jesus was so accessible everywhere He went. He was never unapproachable, irritable, or rude but welcomed sinners into His presence with a humble heart. Enable us to imitate His humility this Christmas season so that others will be drawn to Him as well. Amen.

FRIDAY
Man of Sorrows, Familiar with Suffering

READ

Isaiah 53:1-12

PREPARE

In Isaiah 53, we find one of the most important prophecies about the Messiah. But while it's one of the most important, it's also one of the most difficult to understand. It's hard to wrap our minds around a Savior who came to suffer, a hero who was born to die, and a Messiah "acquainted with grief" (v. 3). In our sinful nature, we resist both recognizing and emulating a humble, suffering King.

But we need to understand that Christ's crucifixion was the prelude to His glorification. The way up for Him was down. And because it was that way for Him, it is that way for His followers too. This is what Jesus means when He says, "The hour has come for the Son of Man to be glorified. Truly, truly, I say to you, unless a grain of wheat falls into the earth and dies, it remains alone; but if it dies, it bears much fruit. Whoever loves his life loses it, and whoever hates his life in this world will keep it for eternal life" (John 12:23-25).

Along with your joys and high points over the last year are also deep valleys of suffering. Your suffering may have resulted from the hurtful behavior of others; it may have occurred because of your own foolish decision-making; or it maybe it's just part of living in a fallen world. But for the Christian, suffering and failure never have the final word. What looks like failure is simply an invitation for restoration, redemption, and hope. This is because of one reason: "Yet it was the will of the Lord to crush him; he has put him to grief. . . . Out of the anguish of his soul he shall see and be satisfied; by his knowledge shall the righteous one, my servant, make many to be accounted righteous" (Isaiah 53:10-11).

Because of the death of Christ for our failures, suffering, and sin, our death is not a payment for our sin but only a dying to sins and an entering into eternal life.[7] Christ's death and acquaintance with sorrow ensures our life and acquaintance with joy (Psalm 16:9-11). Even though He was intimately familiar with suffering, Christ Himself knew that sorrow did not have the final say on His story either. Hebrews 12:2 tells us that He endured the cross for the joy set *before* Him. On His worst day, He knew there was something deeper and richer pulling Him to the joy of another place.

As Augustine reminds us, "Man's Maker was made man that He, Ruler of the stars, might nurse at His mother's breast; that the Bread might hunger, the Fountain thirst, the Light sleep, the Way be tired on its journey; that the Truth might be accused of false witness, the Teacher be beaten with whips, the Foundation be suspended on wood; that Strength might grow weak; that the Healer might be wounded; that Life might die."[8] This week, as we light the Prophet's candle and remember the promises of hope passed down through the ages, remember that because of Jesus, sorrow and suffering do not have the final word on your Advent season, your year, or your story. Jesus was made a man of sorrows so that we might taste the joy of everlasting life.

*

CONSIDER

- How does it bring comfort to you to know that Jesus was "a man of sorrows and acquainted with grief" (Isaiah 53:3)?

- Re-read John 12:23-25. What fruit have you seen come from your suffering?

- Write out a prayer entrusting your sorrows to God, knowing that any grief you endure will be transformed into everlasting joy.

PRAY

Father,

We so quickly forget that just as suffering was a part of Jesus's story, it is an inevitable part of ours. Give us endurance to fix our eyes on the eternal hope we have in the cross and resurrection of Christ. May the joy set before us turn our hearts toward home and prepare us for eternity with You. Amen.

SATURDAY
Healing in His Wings

READ

Malachi 4:1-6

PREPARE

As we come to the end of the first week of Advent, we hear from the book of Malachi. Malachi was the last prophet to speak before the four hundred years of silence between the last stroke of Malachi's pen and the first words of John the Baptist. He writes, "For behold, the day is coming, burning like an oven, when all the arrogant and all evildoers will be stubble. The day that is coming shall set them ablaze, says the Lord of hosts, so that it will leave them neither root nor branch. But for you who fear my name, the sun of righteousness shall rise with healing in its wings. You shall go out leaping like calves from the stall" (Malachi 4:1-2).

This final word from God before the coming of the Word made flesh contains both a warning to the wicked and a promise to the righteous. The warning for the wicked is that the day when Jesus returns will be a day of fire, destruction, fear, and dread. But for those who have put their trust in the Lord, the day of His coming will be a day of jubilation, freedom, healing, and joy. The line that separates the wicked from the righteous is razor thin. Over and over, writers in both the Old and New Testaments are clear: "They have all turned aside; together they have become corrupt; there is none who does good, not even one" (Psalm 14:3; see also Romans 3:10-11). Any righteous response in a human heart is because God seeks us, not the other way around.

But when He seeks us, we all have a choice: We can fear God, like the wicked, and run away from Him. Or we can fear God, like the righteous, and run toward Him. Both the wicked and the righteous are sinners, but only the righteous seek refuge from their sin in repentance and worship of the one true God.

This is the essence of Advent. In our remembering that Christ came and in our waiting for Christ to come again, we have one of two responses to God. We can hide in the dark about our sin, making inadequate excuses and coverings for ourself, just like Adam and Eve (Genesis 3:7-8), or we can be honest about our sin, step into the light of the Son of righteousness, repent, and seek shelter in His covering wings. As Michael Reeves writes, "It is . . . the devil's work to promote a fear of God that makes people afraid of God such that they want to flee from God. The Spirit's work is the exact opposite: to produce in us a wonderful fear that wins and draws us *to* God."[9]

This is the purpose of Malachi's words, then and now: When we see the weight of our sin and experience the loss of life as God meant for it to be on the good earth He created, *we are to fear.* We are to run toward God, recognizing in Him a desire to cover us and heal us, not destroy us. This is why Christ came the first time as the Lamb of God to take away our sin, and this is why He will return again, as the Lamb whose blood ransomed people from every nation for His Father God (John 1:36; Revelation 5:9).

As the first week of Advent draws to a close, draw close to God, and fear. Run toward the Son of righteousness, repent of any sin that stands in the way of your heart and His, and receive the healing His grace alone gives. He does not want your gifts, your perfectly prepared meals, your beautifully decorated homes, or your elaborately orchestrated Christmas pageants; He wants your heart. Fall on your knees, see the Son, and fear. You will discover the only true haven of hope and deliverance is beneath His great and glorious wings.

CONSIDER

- Read Proverbs 1:7. In your own words, explain what it means to fear God.

- What would it look like for you to fear God instead of fearing other people for the remainder of the Christmas season?

- How would fearing God more than anyone or anything else protect, heal, and free your heart?

PRAY

Father,

Thank You for providing hope, healing, and a refuge for us in the Son. Help me run toward Him today, not away from Him; to confess my short-comings and sin; and to find the forgiveness, acceptance, healing, and grace He came to give. Don't let me go through the Christmas season withholding the one thing You truly want—my heart. Amen.

ADVENT
WEEK TWO

THE BETHLEHEM CANDLE: PEACE

THE SECOND SUNDAY OF ADVENT
O Little Town of Bethlehem

Before you begin reading, light two candles on your wreath. The second candle is the Bethlehem Candle, which represents peace.

READ
Micah 5:1-6

PREPARE

Sometime between 725 and 715 BC the prophet Micah foretold that an ancient ruler would arise out of Bethlehem—a ruler who would shepherd His flock in the strength and majesty of the Lord; a ruler who would be the peace and security of His flock. So the Jews waited and waited for the ever-illusive yet ever-longed-for peace. But rather than waiting with their hearts fully surrendered to the Lord, they ran after other gods to look for a peace they could create on their own terms and by doing things their own way.

Because of their disobedience, God sent invading armies and conquerors to bring His rebellious people back into relationship with Him. He sent Nebuchadnezzar the Babylonian, the Medes and the Persians, the Greeks, and finally, He sent the Romans. Although the Israelites repented and turned back to the Lord for short periods of time, they eventually strayed, turning to worship other gods or taking on the culture of their conquerors rather than remaining holy and set apart to the Lord. But a longing for God's promised peace always remained.

After four hundred years of silence—after the final words of the last prophet, Malachi, when the Lord shut the heavens and said no more—the Word became flesh and came to live among us (John 1:14). The Ancient of Days, the ruler whose origins were of old, stepped into time to shepherd His flock. But the peace Israel looked for, the overthrowing of its Roman conquerors, was not the peace Jesus brought. He promised His people He would return one day to put an end to His enemies (Luke 23:28-31), but the victorious King first had to become the sacrificial Lamb.

Colossians 1:19-20 tells us that "For in [Jesus] all the fullness of God was pleased to dwell, and through him to reconcile to himself all things, whether on earth or in heaven, making peace by the blood of his cross." Peace that comes through death on a cross is a very different kind of peace than we normally look for. It's a violent kind of peace. It's a peace that requires a radical repentance that wipes out our sin—a different but deadlier enemy than the Jews expected their ruler to eradicate. But through the cross, peace came. It flowed in a direct line down the path from the manger to the cross at Calvary. But it all began in Bethlehem. So, as you prepare yourself for Christmas this Advent season, don't miss the reason why the Shepherd had to come as the sacrificial Lamb.

He did not come to destroy your physical enemies but to destroy the ultimate enemy who can keep you from spending eternity with the Father. From humble, quiet beginnings in a manger came the peace that passes all understanding; the peace that delivers us from all sin; the peace that gives us a new home, a new nature, and a new name; and the peace that rules hearts and will one day rule the world. Praise God, for our Prince of Peace has come.

CONSIDER

- When was a long-awaited answer you received vastly different than what you expected?

- How Jesus's coming to Bethlehem a different answer to the kind of peace God's people expected?

- What are some ways Jesus promises peace to your heart this Christmas season, even if He allows difficult circumstances to remain?

ADVENT ACTIVITIES

Choose one of the following activities this week to help you remember the peace Jesus brings during this season.

- **Break your patterns.** This can be as simply as choosing a new place to have your quiet time or eating dessert before you have dinner. Every time you do something outside of your daily routine, remind yourself—and any family or friends who might participate—that although God does things differently than we think He should, His way of doing things is always good.

- **Pursue peace everywhere.** Choose to promote peace in your interactions with others, and encourage any family or friends working through this devotional to do the same. Some ideas include being kind to cashiers as you do your Christmas shopping, leaving a snack and thank-you note to those who deliver your packages, and helping your kids or the young people in your life learn to forgive those who have hurt them. If you gather your family or friends to celebrate Jesus during Advent, pray together, asking the Lord to bring true peace on earth in places around the world where there is war, suffering, or people have never heard the name of Jesus. Wherever you are and whatever you do this week, remember that Jesus came into the world to bring peace and we have a part to play in bringing His peace to others.

PRAY

Father,

When You chose to enter the world through the quiet town of Bethlehem so many centuries ago, You chose a humble beginning over a glorious entrance, a life of suffering and sorrow over one of comfort and ease. You chose to give Your people an eternal peace that will never pass away instead of temporary peace that only brings momentary solutions. Thank You for choosing to walk the road from Bethlehem to Calvary. May we learn to take up our cross and follow You on that road to peace, no matter where You lead. As You shepherd our souls, guide us along paths of peace and righteousness for Your name's sake throughout the remainder of the Advent Season. Amen.

CLOSING CAROL:
"O LITTLE TOWN OF BETHLEHEM"

O little town of Bethlehem,
how still we see thee lie!
Above thy deep and dreamless sleep
the silent stars go by.
Yet in thy dark streets shineth
the everlasting light;
the hopes and fears of all the years
are met in thee tonight.

How silently, how silently
the wondrous gift is giv'n!
So God imparts to human hearts
the blessings of His heav'n.
No ear may hear His coming,
but in this world of sin,
where meek souls will receive Him still,
the dear Christ enters in.

O holy Child of Bethlehem,
descend to us, we pray;
cast out our sin, and enter in;
be born in us today.
We hear the Christmas angels,
the great glad tidings tell;
O come to us, abide with us,
our Lord Emmanuel!

MONDAY
House of Bread

READ

Ruth 1:1-22; 4:13-17

PREPARE

Bethlehem was a small, nondescript village on the outskirts of Jerusalem and seems an odd place for the Son of God to be born (Luke 2:4-7). But Bethlehem mattered, and we find one of our first clues about the importance of Bethlehem in the book of Ruth.

Ruth opens with a family traveling away from Bethlehem instead of toward it. Due to a famine, an Israelite family from the tribe of Judah—Elimelech, his wife Naomi, and their two sons—took matters into their own hands to try to fill their stomachs. Instead of relying on God and trusting His providential care for His people, they left the safety of Israel and traveled to Moab, a place of idol worship and rebellion against God.

While there both of their sons married Moabite women—something God's law explicitly commanded His people not to do (Deuteronomy 7:1-4). During their ten-year sojourn in Moab, tragedy struck Elimelech's house, and Naomi was left without husband or sons. She began her journey from Bethlehem with a stomach hungry for bread, but she returned to Bethlehem with an empty, broken heart.

When Naomi returned, her daughter-in-law, Ruth,

committed herself to caring for Naomi, instead of making a way for herself or focusing on her own needs. She traveled to a town that offered no hope of seed for bread or children for a foreign woman outside God's family.

But the writer of Ruth hinted that things are about to change; everything was not as it seemed in Bethlehem, a word in Hebrew that means "house of bread."[10] "And they came to Bethlehem at the beginning of barley harvest" (Ruth 1:22).

This is the essence of Bethlehem: not everyone who mourns will remain bitter. Those who return seeking the living God will be filled.

As the story of Ruth unfolds, we see Naomi receiving a gift in Ruth she did not deserve. Ruth was unflinchingly loyal, supernaturally kind, and courageously obedient to the wishes of her mother-in-law. She gleaned grain in the fields Boaz, a relative of Naomi's deceased husband. And in Boaz, Ruth found a man willing to step in as the family's redeemer.

By the end of the book of Ruth, Naomi was no longer empty but full. Ruth was no longer widowed and childless but married to Boaz and had a son—a son who became the grandfather of King David and was in the direct line of the Messiah, King Jesus.

In John when Jesus says, "I am the bread of life" (John 6:35), He is not saying that we will never experience hunger pains on this earth. Nor is He saying we won't experience tremendous suffering or ache with the pangs of loneliness. But none who come to Him with hungry hearts will remain that way. Worshiping the Child born in Bethlehem ushers in the beginning of a harvest for us all. We serve a Savior who is loyal in His love, unflinching in His covenant commitment to us, and courageously obedient to His Father's commands.

The birth of Christ in Bethlehem was not a random accident; it was a purposeful choice, an announcement that God's love is loyal to us, even though we don't deserve it.

Bethlehem is a promise that we will be filled. When we come to Christ, we might have to endure difficult circumstances, but we don't have to fear being sent away empty-handed. In Christ, the bread of life, we are promised a harvest, and our hands hold more than we could ever dare to believe.

CONSIDER

- In what ways do you feel empty this Advent season?

- How does the story of Ruth and Naomi encourage you to trust that you will not be sent away empty but full?

- Ask today that you would know Jesus as your redeemer. Ask that He would fill every ache with the bread of life only He can give.

PRAY

Father,

Thank You for reminding us through Ruth that even when we stray, You welcome us back to a feast in Your house through Christ. Help us remember the promise from Ruth that Your loyal love will never let us down or send us away empty-handed. In the House of Bethlehem, our hearts can always remain full. Amen.

TUESDAY
A King from Bethlehem

READ
1 Samuel 8:10-9:2; 16:1-13

PREPARE

Unlike the nations around them, Israel was not ruled by a king but by a series of judges. Stuck in a cycle of sin and disobedience during the time of the judges, "everyone did what was right in his own eyes" (Judges 21:25). To grab their attention, God allowed enemies to attack His people, giving them the need for a deliverer and the reminder to cry out to Him. While the deliverer or judge would restore Israel's relationship with God for a time, the people soon returned to their idolatrous, wicked ways.

In the opening chapters of 1 Samuel, Israel was overrun by the Philistines. Instead of crying out to God to deliver them, they cried out for an earthly king to rule over them. The prophet Samuel was grieved because he knew an earthly king would only increase Israel's troubles (1 Samuel 8:10-18). But God told Samuel, "Obey their voice and make them a king" (1 Samuel 8:22), and under God's leading, Samuel anointed Saul as Israel's first king.

Saul was everything the people of Israel wanted—wealthy, tall, handsome. But Saul was intent on doing things his way instead of God's way and was in danger of leading Israel back into captivity. So, God rejected Saul and chose another as king in his place (1 Samuel 15:26, 28).

God sent Samuel to anoint His kind of king: a man after God's own heart. It's not hard for us to guess where God sent Samuel to find him. He told Samuel, "I will send you to Jesse *the Bethlehemite*, for I have provided for myself a king among his sons" (1 Samuel 16:1, emphasis added).

Seven of Jesse's sons passed in front of Samuel's penetrating gaze. They looked like kings, but God told Samuel, "Do not look on his appearance or on the height of his stature, because I have rejected him. For the Lord sees not as man sees: man looks on the outward appearance, but the Lord looks on the heart" (1 Samuel 16:7). As a last resort, Jesse called in his youngest son from the sheep fields. David did not look like a king people would follow. He was the youngest of his brothers, a word in Hebrew that means "diminutive, less, least."[11] But God did not care about David's physical stature: He saw David's heart. He saw a king who would not be perfect but who would be repentant. He saw a king who would run toward God, not for the gifts God would give him but the sake of God's character and steadfast love.

Almost a thousand years later under the same Bethlehem skies, Mary gave birth to her first-born son and called Him Jesus, just as the angel had commanded. Only a few people— some smelly shepherds straight out of the fields of tending the temple sheep—recognized the event of His birth. Most people missed him. Everyone was looking for a tall, handsome, strong king of Israel who could defeat the enemy of Rome. No one was expecting an infant king to be born in Bethlehem to a teenage girl and a humble carpenter.

But Israel was in disarray and did not need just any king but the Shepherd-King, who would lead the flocks of Israel to safety and security in the fear of the Lord and the comfort of the Spirit. This is what Bethlehem teaches us today: if things don't look like you thought they would or want them to, close your eyes so you can really see. Although we are tempted to judge from the outward appearance of things, the Lord looks at the heart. And there's no telling what He will still do with those whose hearts are fully His.

CONSIDER

- What situation or person in your life are you tempted to look at and judge from the outer appearance instead of the heart?

- How does the selection of Saul contrasted to the selection of David help you to see things from a different perspective?

- This Advent season, ask that God would give you a heart like David and like Jesus, your Shepherd-King, who will do all His will and serve His purpose in your generation (Acts 13:22, 36).

PRAY

Father,

Thank You for giving us the king in Jesus we needed instead of the king we wanted. Forgive us for looking at the outward appearance instead of the heart. Please help us to see as You do and recognize our Savior, Shepherd, and King as He moves among us today. May we choose to embrace humility on the road to Bethlehem as we worship, follow, and serve Him as our King. Amen.

WEDNESDAY
A House of Grace

READ

2 Samuel 7:1-17

PREPARE

As we continue down the road to Bethlehem this Advent season, the next stop is God's covenant with David in 2 Samuel 7. As Israel's king, David had fought more wars against the enemies of God than he can count. He had provided peace for the people of Israel, helping them expand their borders into more of the land God promised to them. He brought the ark of the covenant from the house of Obed-edom to Jerusalem, Israel's capital city, and built a palace for himself. But now he wanted to move the ark from a temporary tent to a permanent dwelling place.

At first glance, David's request sounds noble and self-less. He wanted to take his time and finances to build a house for God. But through the prophet Nathan, God told David no. Instead, *He* would be the one to build David a house and an everlasting kingdom, not the other way around.

Behind all our good intentions to do something great for God lies the temptation to earn His favor or get into His good graces through the works of our hands. But God is adamant: any favor, gift, blessing, or grace we receive is not through our own merit. We don't earn God's favor or grace. He freely gives it to us because of who He is. This is because He knows anything we worked to earn from Him we could never keep; we would always be in danger of losing His favor if gaining it was based on our own merit or performance.

As David learned about himself just four chapters later, even the "great ones of the earth" fall (2 Samuel 7:9). He committed adultery with Bathsheba, the wife of one of his loyal servants and friends, and then ordered his friend to be murdered to cover up his affair. In David's confession in Psalm 51, he cried out, "Behold, I was brought forth in iniquity, and in sin did my mother conceive me" (Psalm 51:5). David discovered something we all must discover about ourselves: His crime "was no freak event: it was in character; an extreme expression of the warped creature he had always been, and of the faulty stock he sprang from."[12]

This is why 2 Samuel 7 is so foundational to everything we understand about God's covenant promises to David and the people of God. A descendant from David's house will forever rest on David's throne because of grace and grace alone. God's promise to David did not fail when David failed; it stood firm on the faithful character of God.

Let this truth sink into your heart today: Christmas does not come to you this year because your good deeds outweigh your bad ones. David's descendant does not reign on the throne of your heart because you have kept up your end of the bargain with God. We all fail daily. But God's Word never fails, and His promises are sure. Not only did He build David a house, but He has built you a house as well (John 14:1-3, 23). And since you did not earn this house, you cannot fail to receive it because of the faithfulness of God.

Go back to 2 Samuel 7 and read through God's extraordinary promises to David once again. As you read, know that through Christ, the baby born in Bethlehem, those are promises for you as well. The apostle Peter says it this way: "But you are a chosen race, a royal priesthood, a holy nation, a people for his own possession, that you may proclaim the excellencies of him who called you out of darkness into his marvelous light" (1 Peter 2:9). Receive the sure promise of the Son of David this Christmas season, knowing you serve a good and gracious God.

CONSIDER
- How do you resist the gift of grace and try to earn favor with God?

- Instead of working to build a perfect Christmas for yourself and the people around you, how can you stop and receive the gift of Christmas that has already been given?

- What is a practical response you can have today for other people around you, especially those in your very own household, when they have need for grace?

PRAY
Father,
Grace changes us. It levels the playing field and helps us understand kings and shepherds alike are all dependent on grace. We do not receive Your favor this Christmas because we deserve it. Rather, we have Your favor because Your character alone upholds it. Don't let us resist grace by continuing to try to earn Your love. Let us receive grace this Advent season and then give it to others freely as well. Amen.

THURSDAY
Refuge in the King

READ

Psalm 2:1-12

PREPARE

The book of Psalms has been compared to "a literary sanctuary."[13] Through 150 different songs, we are taught how to worship God while navigating every emotion of the human heart. Psalms 1–2 are known as the gatekeeper psalms.[14] They show us the appropriate heart posture for those who want to enter the sanctuary of the Lord. While Psalm 1 reminds us we are to give our full "attention to the Word of God," Psalm 2 instructs us we are to live life in constant reverence and submission to the Son of God.[15]

Psalm 2 was written as a coronation psalm for Israel's kings in David's line, which, as we learned yesterday, God promised would last forever. But by the time the last kings of Israel and Judah were carried off into captivity, no one from David's line had ever fully fit the description of this king. One greater than David or his son Solomon was needed "to justify the full fury of these threats and the glory of these promises" found in the psalm.[16] This could only mean one of two things: either God failed to keep His promise to David, or this psalm was talking about a king who was yet to come.

Only with David's heir ultimately being King Jesus does Psalm 2 make sense. When the kings of the earth gathered against Christ—the Greek word that means "anointed" or "the Messiah"[17]—God's response "to human pride and power" was to set His King on Zion, His holy hill (Psalm 2:6).[18] In Acts 4:25-28, Peter and John use Psalm 2 to describe the events of Christ's trial and crucifixion. Going to Zion meant that the Anointed One was crucified for our sins. But death was not the end of His story. In Acts 13:33, Paul used Psalm 2:7 to describe the resurrection: "Let it be known to you therefore, brothers, that through this man forgiveness of sins is proclaimed to you, and by him everyone who believes is freed" (Acts 13:38-39).

As each one of us enters the sanctuary to worship Christ this Advent season, we have a choice: We can rage against and resist God's rule in our lives like the kings and rulers of the earth in Jesus's day and in our day as well, or we can "kiss the Son," a phrase that means "to pay true homage" to Him through our trust, obedience, and rest.[19] For while Jesus came the first time to die for His enemies, He will return to make all wrongs right. None of us knows the day when He will return nor do we know the moment we will take our last breath. Like the psalmist of old, we must remember, "there is no *refuge* from [God]: only *in him*."[20]

A King who was willing to lay aside His glory, come humbly as a baby, live obediently as a man, and die willingly for His enemies is a King worth bending your knee to. Remember, Advent is not just about looking back and remembering that Christ came, it is about looking ahead and remembering that He will come again. So don't delay in giving the Savior from Bethlehem, David's heir and king, your full worship as you enter the sanctuary. Through the written Word, remain wholly devoted to the living Word, finding refuge, safety, and security in Him.

CONSIDER

- How have you found yourself resisting the rule of God in your life?

- What are some ways God has invited you to take refuge in His Son this Advent season?

- Where can you make time to study the written Word of God while you commune with the living Word a priority beyond the Advent season?

PRAY

Father,

The rulers of this world still rage against Your Anointed One. My heart resists Your rule when I want to walk my own way instead of the way I read about in Your Word. When I resist Your good and holy rule in my life, quicken my heart to repent and find refuge in Jesus. Remind me He is a King who did not come to punish His enemies but to die for them, and He waits patiently for all hearts to pay homage to His Holy Name. Amen.

FRIDAY
Jesse's Family Tree

READ

Isaiah 11:1-16

PREPARE

At the time of Isaiah's prophecy, the family of Jesse was exactly like a stump: fruitless, branchless, and barren. The kings of Israel from David's line had turned away from worship of the living God. The Israelite people to whom Isaiah is sent "were heirs of great promises but appear to have forfeited them."[21] In the first five chapters of Isaiah, darkness had closed in on God's people through their wandering and waywardness. But then, a light began to dawn.

But how? How does grace bloom from barrenness? How does fruit sprout from a dried-up stump? There is only one explanation: a "secret vitality" pulses underneath the roots of Jesse's family tree.[22] This power and presence is not only the shoot *from* Jesse (Isaiah 11:1) but also the root from which Jesse *comes* (Isaiah 11:10). Dietrich Bonhoeffer puts it this way: "Life in a prison cell may well be compared to Advent: one waits, hopes, and does this, that, or the other—things that are really of no consequence—the door is shut, and can only be opened *from the outside*."[23] Israel's help and hope as well as our help and hope must come from something outside our failed promises, barren hearts, splintered relationships, and fractured lives. A secret vitality, a powerful presence must help us from the outside.

This is what Isaiah sees: a branch blooming, a root renewing, a garden flourishing, a people gathering who are all running toward a perfect king. In verses 2-5, we see a King's character fueled by the power of the Spirit. He is wise and understanding and "has the ability to see to the heart of an issue."[24] He can "devise a right course of action," and he also has the power to carry His actions through.[25] He enjoys an intimate, personal relationship with the Lord and lives in the fear of the Lord, running ever toward Him, not away from Him.

In verses 6-9, we see that not only does this King have perfect character, but His rule and reign also produce a new order in the natural world. The curse of "enmity" between the serpent and the seed of the woman is lifted (Genesis 3:15), and Eden's goodness, created order, and beauty is restored.

This King also restores peace and flourishing in the relational world. In a second exodus, the root of Jesse draws all the peoples of the earth to Himself (vv.10-11), and as He gathers, He restores. Jealousy and actions of hostility are not allowed to wreak havoc on the united people of God (vv. 12-13).[26]

All this from a dry stump. All this flourishing from a family line perishing. All this hope, joy, and peace from a King who broke into our barrenness from the outside in. Like we learned earlier this week, a flourishing life does not come to us because we earn it or deserve it. Our inward renewal is a not a reward for our good behavior. It is a gift of grace from a good and gracious King.

This Advent season, your life and your family may resemble more of a dry stump than a fruitful vine. But the same King who came to Bethlehem, who lived and died to set you free to flourish, comes for you this Christmas. He will not always give you blooming, flourishing circumstances, but He will walk with you to give you a flourishing heart. As branches from the root of our fruitful King, trust that you will bear much fruit as you wait expectantly for His coming (John 15:5).

CONSIDER

- What circumstances in your life appear to be withered or hopeless right now?

- How does knowing your help does not depend on you or your circumstances but comes from the outside in through your perfect King give you peace this Christmas season?

- What would it look like for you to bear fruit in whatever circumstances feel less than flourishing? For help answering this question, read Galatians 5:22-23, then ask the Spirit of God for His supernatural help in bearing this kind of fruit.

PRAY

Father,

You not only gave us Your Son, but through Christ, You also give us Your Spirit. Since we live by the Spirit, help us to keep in step with the Him (Galatians 5:25), bearing fruit as we learn to wait for and abide in the root of Jesse, David's son and king. Amen.

SATURDAY
The Long Wait

READ

Matthew 1:1-17

PREPARE

All week we have walked Bethlehem's road, waiting and wondering if we will ever meet David's King. But just when we think all hope is lost, we read, "The book of the genealogy of Jesus Christ, *the son of David*, the son of Abraham" (Matthew 1:1, emphasis added). There He is in human form, David's son, yet ancient of days. He really, truly came.

Pause in that for just a moment. God's promise to David to build him a forever kingdom came over one thousand years before Matthew penned his first line. I have a hard time trusting God will fulfill a promise from His Word to me if I have to wait longer than ten months, much less ten years. But a thousand? I think after David's affair, Solomon's idolatry, Ahaz's apostasy, and Manasseh's wickedness I would have walked away from believing God would keep His promise, much less *wanted* to keep His promise.

But in the fullness of time, the Son of David came, willingly identifying Himself with a family whose ancestors included murderers, deceivers, adulterers, polygamists, scoffers, and downright evildoers (Galatians 4:4).

He didn't come to tell us to get our act together or condemn us to our fate, He came to live among us. He stepped into family baggage and a dark family history. He did not bring a heavenly host to protect Him from disease or sickness, betrayal or abandonment, disappointment or disillusionment, or unkind words. He walked here on earth with obedience to His Father as His protection and daily dependence on the Spirit as His refuge and shield.

Think about something you're waiting on. Does God's response seem slow? Does He seem absolutely unwilling to act or maybe even unable to hear? God came through on the enormity of His promises to David, and He will be faithful to fulfill His promises to you too (Romans 8:31-32).

Each name in Jesus's genealogy was a signpost of grace on the road to Bethlehem; part of the perfect prelude God wrote for the entrance for His Son. By the time Jesus was born to "Joseph the husband of Mary" (Matthew 1:16), all human hope for a Savior had dried up. Not just because of the passage of time but because of the people's failure to uphold their end of the covenant with God. When that was abundantly clear, God came. He waited so that anyone who reads the record of Christ knows His coming was the overflow of God's mercy and grace.

Matthew tells us there were six cycles of seven generations before the coming of Jesus. When Christ was born to Joseph and Mary, He was the seventh seven after a long line of sinners. This is significant because throughout Scripture, seven is the number that represents "the perfect, complete work of God."[27] In no uncertain language, Matthew pointed out God knew what He was doing all along. When the way was dark, the branches barren, and the people of God thought they had been long forgotten, the perfect Prince of Peace appeared.

So don't give up waiting on the fulfillment of the promises of God. "For all the promises of God find their Yes in [Jesus]," and He has placed His Spirit "in our hearts as the guarantee" (2 Corinthians 1:20, 22). The night may be dark, and the road may be long, but Christ always comes to those who patiently wait for Him. May your heart take courage this Christmas season, no matter how long your wait.

CONSIDER
- What promise from God's Word are you tempted to think God has *forgotten* to fulfill?

- How does the genealogy of Christ offer hope and peace to your heart as you wait?

- What is one specific name from Christ's family tree that reminds you to wait in trust that God has not forgotten you but will be faithful?

PRAY
Father,
We all are waiting on something, and we have all probably wondered if You have forgotten to keep Your promises. Thank You for the reminder that You never forget. Once You promise, You will always do exactly what You say. Give us hope and courage to wait in the winter of Advent for the renewal, hope, and peace Jesus brings. Amen.

ADVENT
WEEK THREE

THE SHEPHERD'S CANDLE: JOY

THE THIRD SUNDAY OF ADVENT
Joy to the World

Before you begin reading, light three candles on your wreath. The third candle is the Shepherd's Candle, which represents joy.

READ
Luke 2:8-21

PREPARE
It's the third Sunday of Advent, and the countdown to Christmas is already halfway over. We are halfway through fighting the madness of the Christmas crowds, going to one more Christmas party, decorating one more Christmas cookie, buying one more Christmas present, and addressing one last Christmas card. The countdown to Christmas can be incredibly joyful and exciting, but it can also be completely exhausting and overwhelming. How do we maintain joy during a busy Christmas season?

Let's start by pausing today to consider the shepherds. Pause to enter their world of sheep, smells, and late nights on quiet hillsides. Pause to consider that on the night of Christ's birth was an incredibly ordinary night for the shepherds, just as most of your nights are. They were working the same job, herding the same sheep, surrounded by the same people. And

then, in a moment, the night sky was filled with heavenly be-
ings proclaiming the glorious birth of Israel's long-awaited King.
An ordinary night was filled with the surprising gift of the extraordinary, the divine invaded earth, and these average, ordinary shepherds were never the same.

Visitations from angels, not to mention an entire host
of angels, often left people in the Old and New Testaments
filled with dread, having lost the ability to speak as well as
walk or even stand. But this visitation was different. This visitation filled the shepherds with a holy joy that pushed them
out of the worries and cares of the everyday into the mystery
and majesty of God with us. If the shepherds had worries or
cares that evening, we can assume their worrying ceased. If
the shepherds had fears or their hopes in the faithfulness of
God had dwindled, we can rest assured their hopes were re-
kindled. They saw the glory of God in human form, swaddled
and lying in a manger.

So, pause to consider the joy of the shepherds. Stop
amid your Christmas countdown to run with the shepherds to
the stable, stoop to enter the low entrance of a cave cut out
of a hillside, and peer over the edge of a rough-hewn feeding
trough filled with glory. Then, worship. Don't let your to-do list,
or schoolwork, or messy desk work steal your joy; stop long
enough to allow the gift of His arrival to transform your ordinary evening into an opportunity for awe, wonder, and joy. As
you do so, like the shepherds, your worries, cares, and exhaus-
tion from Christmas will have no other option but to disappear.

If you and I can consider Jesus's birth and its meaning,
praising God for sending His Son for us, every day between now
and Christmas, we will have taken care of the most important
part of our preparation. We can walk through the remainder of
the Advent season with the supernatural peace and holy joy
that only comes when we pause to ponder and worship Jesus.

CONSIDER

- What's threatening to steal your joy as you think about the week ahead?

- How does worship of Jesus transform your worry into trust, peace, hope, and joy?

- This week, when you begin to feel anxious, what is one practical way you can stop, pay attention to your worry, give it to Jesus, and then worship, expressing gratitude to God that Jesus came and is coming again (Philippians 4:4-7)?

ADVENT ACTIVITIES

Choose one of the following activities this week to help you remember the joy Jesus brings during this season.

- **Remember a gift.** With your family or a group of friends, discuss a gift you received that you really wanted. Then consider the following: Do you still have that item? Do you still use it? Does that gift still bring you joy? The truth is, no gift lasts forever except the best Christmas gift we've ever received: Jesus. He lasts forever, and anything He gives to us, including joy, lasts forever too.

- **Give together.** Gather with a group of friends or family and do something to bring others joy. Here are a few ideas:
    - Make cookies and decorate them, then deliver them to someone who needs a taste of joy this Christmas season.
    - Visit people in a local hospital or nursing home who won't be able to get out on their own for the holidays. Consider singing Christmas carols if it's allowed.
    - Buy a cheap mug and fill it with a candy cane and a packet of hot chocolate mix. Hand write an invitation to your Christmas Eve service and tie it to the mug handle with a ribbon. Deliver it to someone new!
    - Set aside some of the money you would normally spend on gifts for one another and use that money to buy a gift of clothes or food for a needy family in your community and deliver them together.

PRAY
Father,
During the hurry and rush of the Christmas season, we take time today to run with the shepherds to the manger. As we worship Christ, may our awe and wonder wipe away all our worries and sorrow. Throughout the remainder of the Advent season, remind us that even our most mundane tasks and moments can be infused with joy as we consider the mystery of our Savior, who is Christ the Lord. Amen.

CLOSING CAROL:
"JOY TO THE WORLD!"

Joy to the World, the Lord is come!
Let earth receive her King!
Let every heart prepare Him room,
and heav'n and nature sing,
and heav'n and nature sing,
and heav'n, and heav'n and nature sing.

Joy to the earth, the Savior reigns!
Let men their songs employ,
while fields and floods, rocks, hills, and plains
repeat the sounding joy,
repeat the sounding joy,
repeat, repeat the sounding joy.

No more let sins and sorrows grow,
nor thorns infest the ground;
He comes to make His blessings flow
far as the curse is found,
far as the curse is found,
far as, far as the curse is found.

He rules the world with truth and grace,
and makes the nations prove
the glories of His righteousness
and wonders of His love,
and wonders of His love,
and wonders, wonders of His love.

MONDAY
The Joy of Limits

READ

Luke 2:1-7; Philippians 2:5-11

PREPARE

When I find myself stressed and overwhelmed by the demands of a season that is supposed to bring joy, I have to remember to pause, step back, and separate the cultural threads that become tangled up in to the biblical threads of Christmas. While the goal of every Christ follower is to exalt Christ throughout the Christmas season, we often become distracted by the cries and demands of our culture. Our culture ignores the good limits that God has given us, limits that include our needs to sleep, pay attention to only one thing at a time, and be in only one place at a time.

As we see in both Luke 2 and Philippians 2, when Christ came to this earth, He did not ignore His human limits but embraced them. Christ was fully God, but He always perfectly, obediently lived within the limits of being fully human. He slept when He was exhausted, sat down and rested when He was weary, ate when He was hungry, and ministered to people one person and one situation at a time. He never did anything without keeping in perfect step with the limits His heavenly Father ordained for Him (John 5:19).

We can maintain our good, God-given limits this Christmas by remembering God is not disappointed by our inability to always be all things to all people. He is not frustrated with you because you can't exceed the limits of time, spend money that you do not have, bypass the need for sleep, or focus on more than one thing or person at a time. We can also set our limits and then make our calendars, shopping lists, and commitments within the boundaries of those limits instead of committing first and then frantically trying to fit it all in.

When God created Adam and Eve, a twenty-four-hour day, rest, food, diligent work, relational intimacy with one another, and healthy dependence on God were all part of the good limits He wove into the fabric of creation before the fall. We must remember, as Eve failed to do, that not all limits are sinful; they are necessary for flourishing and living full, obedient, and dependent lives in relational intimacy with Him.

So today, slow down long enough to consider your God-ordained limits. When Christ took on flesh and dwelt among us (John 1:14), the joy of Christmas was celebrated and fully realized through Christ leaning into His limits, not resisting them. He did not resist the limits of a womb and a messy, pain-filled entrance into a weary world. He did not resist the limits of infancy with an ongoing need for sleep and a mother's supply of milk. As He grew, He did not resist His limits in obedience as a son or dependence on His parent's care. And because He did not resist His limits, He grew in wisdom, stature, and favor with God and with others, becoming all God desired for Him to be (Luke 2:51-52; Hebrews 5:8-9).

During a season and in a culture that pushes us to ignore our limits, quiet your heart by acknowledging, embracing, trusting, and even celebrating your limits as God's blessed child under His good, protective care. As you do so, you will draw on the all-sufficient and power your limitless God provides. When we give up the expectation to be all things to all people and limit ourselves to trust and obey our good God, our hearts can rest, find joy, and prepare the way for Christ this Christmas season. Just as He grew and flourished in His limits, so will we.

CONSIDER

- What limits in your life are you ignoring or frustrated by this Christmas season?

- What would you need to give up to live within your limits?

- Does giving up certain things during the Christmas season make you nervous or afraid? If so, why? What are you afraid you will miss, or who are you afraid you will disappoint?

- Write out a prayer thanking God for the good limits He wove into your life. Repent for living beyond those limits and ask Him for the strength and courage to live in full dependence on Him as your good Father, just as Jesus did. Trust that life within those limits is flourishing and full of joy.

PRAY

Father,

Letting go of my limits is frightening. I am afraid of disappointing people around me, including myself. Quiet my heart with the reminder that Your limits are good, and whatever I release in obedience to Your Word and Your ways I will gain in right relationship with You and others. Amen.

TUESDAY
The Gift of Grace

READ

Luke 1:5-25

PREPARE

As we turn to Luke 1, the first major characters we encounter in the Christmas story are an elderly priest and his wife, Zechariah and Elizabeth. God promised this barren couple a son who would prepare the way for God's promised King.

At first, Zechariah struggled with the angel Gabriel's announcement of good news. Perhaps he thought it was too preposterous, too much like Abraham and Sarah's story. The birth of Isaac was thousands of years before, and encounters with angels, flaming torches, and burning bushes were a thing of the past. But after years of silence from the mouth of God, the angel announced God was going to do the impossible, despite Zechariah's unbelief.

Advent arrives during a cold, wintry time of year. The air is chilled, the trees are bare, and the predominant color is grey. But joy runs deep in Advent's soil, for God still promises barren and broken hearts that He has not forgotten them. He came to Zechariah when he least expected it, and He still comes. God still speaks to things that are not and calls them as though they were: stubborn spouses, rebellious children, broken homes, and bruised hearts become redeemed, restored, rebuilt, holy, and loved (Romans 4:17).

But Advent also reminds us God's grace doesn't depend on our hearts' ability to muster up enough faith to believe; it depends only on God's graciousness to remember His promises and help us receive. When Gabriel appeared to Zechariah, the priest was standing in the temple burning incense at the hour of prayer, feet away from the presence of the living God in the holy of holies. But while his lips were praying, his heart was unbelieving. While Zechariah's words are uttered without real hope of receiving an answer, God's gift is still given.

Can you relate to praying by rote, obeying, and going through the motions when you don't really believe? As we've seen throughout the Advent story, Christmas does not come to us because we earn it, deserve it, or pray the right prayers to invoke it. Christmas comes because God never fails to keep His promises, even when we've let go of hope that He will.

Zechariah's righteous living, praying, and then surprise at God's answering reminds me of a letter from John Newton to a parishioner: "When you cannot see your way, be satisfied that He is your leader. When your spirit is overwhelmed within you, He knows your path; He will not leave you to sink. He has appointed seasons of refreshment, and you shall find He does not forget you. Above all, keep close to the throne of grace. If we seem to get no good by attempting to draw near Him we may be sure we shall get none by keeping away from Him."[28]

We don't walk blamelessly and righteously before God in hopes that He will give us what we want. Our righteous living, obedient serving, and humble praying is to help us remember God's promises and to stay close to God Himself. *He* is our reward. While He may not give us what we want exactly when we want it, He will always give more than we ever dared to believe according to all the promises found in His Word.

Take time this Advent season to discover how things that are "not" can become as if they "were" when, despite our unbelieving hearts, God speaks and draws near. In His presence, barrenness still blooms and death becomes life, sometimes in our circumstances in the here and now but always in our hearts.

CONSIDER

- What prayers do you pray you don't really believe God will answer?

- John Newton said, "All shall work together for good; everything is needful that He sends; nothing can be needful that He withholds."[29] Is this something you truly believe? Why or why not?

- Read and write out the description of God in Romans 4:17, and then ask God to help your unbelief and heal your heart this Christmas season.

PRAY

Father,

We do not understand why hopelessness and despair often seem to have the last word in our lives. Like Zechariah, help us to stay near the throne of grace in our time of need, trusting You are the God who heals our hearts, and helps us in our time of need (Hebrews 4:16). Amen.

WEDNESDAY
Overshadowed

READ

Luke 1:26-38

PREPARE

In Luke 1, the first major character we encounter after Zechariah and Elizabeth is Mary, the mother of Jesus. Unlike Zechariah's doubtful response to the angel, Mary's response was full of humility and faith. Nevertheless, she still had valid questions. Gabriel's reply is as mysterious as it is informative: "The Holy Spirit will come upon you, and the power of the Most High will overshadow you" (Luke 1:35).

Similar words were used in the book of Exodus as God gave Moses instructions for building the ark of the covenant:

- "You shall make a mercy seat of pure gold" (Exodus 25:17).
- "And you shall make two cherubim of gold; of hammered work shall you make them, on the two ends of the mercy seat" (Exodus 25:18).
- "The cherubim shall spread out their wings above, overshadowing the mercy seat with their wings, their faces one to another" (Exodus 25:20).
- "There I will meet with you, and from above the mercy seat, from between the two cherubim that are on the

ark of the testimony, I will speak with you about all that I will give you in commandment for the people of Israel" (Exodus 25:22).

In the tabernacle, God chose to meet with His people under the shadow of the cherubim's outstretched wings. Several thousand years later, when God became flesh to dwell among us, He began His journey by overshadowing a woman's womb. In the Old Testament, standing in the presence of the Almighty meant certain death. Anyone who entered the holy of holies, except the High Priest once a year, immediately died. Anyone who even touched the ark died as well (1 Samuel 6:19; 2 Samuel 6:6-7). Yet Mary's womb was a safe resting place for the shadow of the Almighty; the shadow that had been so mysterious and full of dread in ages past now brought forth the life and light the world had been waiting for.

God's dwelling place is no longer inaccessible. His shadow became our refuge when it brought forth Immanuel, God with us, and His shadow remains the safest place on earth. To be the mother of the Messiah was a privilege reserved only for one woman, but we are all invited to enter the shadow of the Almighty. The author of Psalm 91 writes to us, "He who dwells in the shelter of the Most High will abide in the shadow of the Almighty. I will say to the Lord, 'My refuge and my fortress, my God, in whom I trust'" (Psalm 91:1-2).

This is the message of Advent and the Christmas season: through the overshadowing of Mary's womb, Christ was born, and God has drawn near; through the death and resurrection of Christ, our sin has been removed, and we can safely rest in His shadow; and through His second coming, the shadows of this earth will disappear, and we will see Him face-to-face (1 Corinthians 13:12). Until then, we wait. Come, Lord Jesus, come.

CONSIDER

- In Old Testament times, why do you think it was so dangerous to approach the presence of God in the holy of holies (Leviticus 16:15-16)?

- Read Hebrews 10:19-22. Why do we have confidence now to enter the holy place and abide in the shadow of holy God?

- This Christmas season, how can your life reflect the confidence, assurance, and peace that comes from abiding in God's shadow?

PRAY

Father,

For thousands of years, standing in the shadow of Your presence was a privilege reserved only for a few people. But You chose to make Your presence accessible to all who love You. Thank You for allowing us to live in Your shadow, a place of atonement, protection, refuge, comfort, and peace (Hebrews 10:19-22). May we use these remainder of the advent season to draw close and abide in your shadow. Amen.

THURSDAY
Favored One

READ

Luke 1:26-33

PREPARE

Centuries have passed, but people from every generation have thought of Mary as supremely blessed. Today, as our thoughts turn to Mary, it's easy to imagine her walking the streets of Nazareth shrouded with a cloud of glory so that all who encountered her knew of her favored status.

But the reality of life for Mary was quite different from most of our imaginings. No one else besides Zechariah and Elizabeth had the inside information about the baby growing inside of Mary's womb. She knew she was a virgin, and Joseph knew she was a virgin, but did anyone else? Scripture suggests that rumors never stopped circulating that Mary had given birth to an illegitimate son (John 8:41). This seems like strange and unfair treatment for a woman who was greeted by Gabriel himself as one favored by God.

Mary's life reminds us God's favor usually doesn't give us the life we want. We imagine receiving God's favor means basking in human greatness and earthly glory, but it often means loss of reputation, a good name, and a comfortable life. When we ask God for His favor, we usually mean we want favorable circumstances and the favor of people, but we are really asking God to interfere in our lives to make us holy rather than happy.

When God gives us favor, He often gives us the gift of humility to go along with it to keep us from an inflated view of ourselves and wholly dependent on Him. Like Mary, humility can come in the form of humiliation and a loss of reputation and a good name. Humility can also come in the form of sickness, a physical handicap, a difficult relationship, financial loss or ruin, or shattered dreams of life looking the way we thought it would.

The question is, will we have courage like Mary to keep our eyes on Jesus and trust that His ways are not our ways but are better? Will we have the strength to leave the defense of our reputation and good name to God, trusting He will make all things right in the end?

Living life obediently according to God's Word meant much suffering for Mary—and not just during her unexplained pregnancy. She watched Jesus skyrocket to popularity and fame and then fall dramatically from favor as He was tried and crucified as a common criminal. She stood close to the cross of her Son's broken body, experiencing loss as only a mother can, and when she gained Him back through the resurrection, she lost Him again in the ascension. She would have to wait, with a mother's ache in her heart, to hold Him in her arms and see Him face-to-face again. When God chose Mary, He knew His Son would not just need a mother who was humble, gentle, hospitable, and gracious, He knew Jesus would need a mother who suffered well and modeled how to entrust all of life into God's hands.

Like Mary, can we count it a blessing to be in the shadow of the Most High, even if it means losing our comfortable, predictable life in the process? Like Mary, can we be willing to live for the favor of God even if it means losing the favor of man? May God give us the grace to not only embrace the favor and good gifts He gives but also the humility and trust necessary to go along with them. Like Mary, this humility is what will make us truly great.

CONSIDER

- When have you sensed God's favor in your life?

- How have humbling or humiliating circumstances accompanied His favor?

- How have those circumstances kept you dependent on God and drawn you into an even closer and deeper relationship with Him?

PRAY

Father,

Thank You for the example of a young girl from Nazareth. Forgive us for wanting Your favor only to increase our reputation and good name. We pray that when Your favor shines on us, we'll use it to glorify You and grow Your kingdom. May we suffer well through the humbling circumstances You allow, trusting the grace and goodness You always give. Amen.

FRIDAY
Mary's Song

READ

Luke 1:39-56

PREPARE

Mary's spontaneous reply to her relative Elizabeth's praise is one of the most beautiful songs in all of Scripture. There was no dress rehearsal for this song and no prompting from an offstage script. It was simply the cry of Mary's heart, a spontaneous over-flow of the joy of the Lord. Within this song are at least thirty different references to Old Testament passages, and over half of them were from the Psalms. Jesus said, "out of the abundance of the heart [the] mouth speaks" (Luke 6:45), and we can see that although the Word indwelled Mary physically, the Word was an integral part of her very being.

Notice that while the first few lines of Mary's song refer to herself and the greatness of God in her life, most of the song magnifies God. Mary knew the coming of the Messiah had noth-ing to do with her abilities but was about God's character and faithfulness to His covenant promises to His children. Every reader of Mary's song encounters the character of God Himself and sees His holiness, mercy, generosity, and might. The reader also walks away knowing how to approach God: with fear and reverence, humility, hunger, poverty of spirit, and confidence in God's willingness to uphold His promises.

By all measures, Mary was poor by the world's standards. She did not have much to offer Jesus in the way of material possessions or social opportunities or advantages. But her heart was of great worth. Her song shows she was rich in the knowledge and fear of the Lord. And as we learned with God's selection of David as Israel's king, "the Lord sees not as man sees: man looks on the outward appearance, but the Lord looks on the heart" (1 Samuel 16:7).

Jesus often quoted the Psalms during His ministry. Jesus knew the Psalms well. So did Mary. It's reasonable to assume that in raising Jesus, Mary passed on her love of and devotion to the Psalms and the Hebrew Bible more broadly to her oldest son. As we get to know Mary, we can begin to see why God chose her. He knew she would teach Jesus how to tie His sandals and when to say please and thank you. But she would also, as Proverbs 10:21 says, feed and nourish her Son with the Word of God and show Him how to use the Psalms as a "medicine chest" for His heart and "the best possible guide for practical living."[30]

The temptation at Christmas is to think we need to give our children and the people we love lavish, expensive gifts. Expensive gifts might be fun for a moment, but the real, lasting treasure is the Word of God. The best gift you and I can give to our families and friends this Christmas season are a life lived according to God's Word and words that flow from a heart steeped in God's Word. The point is not to just memorize verses but to meditate on them and live them out.

Our families and friends don't need more social advantages or opportunities or trips or tennis shoes or clothing; they need people in their lives who love God's Word, spend time thinking about God's Word, and then live it out in front of them.

We won't always know the plans and purposes God has for us. When given the opportunity to promote herself or praise God, Mary was ready. We can be ready too by storing His Word in our hearts, so that when surprises come—whether joyful or sorrowful—our hearts will overflow with more than just poetic language. They will point all who look to us to magnify the One within and reveal a heart of great worth.

CONSIDER

- Read Proverbs 10:20-21, and then think for a moment: what do your words reveal about your heart?

- Is reading, thinking about, and praying God's Word a regular part of your life? Why or why not? If not, how can it be?

- What would it look like for you to give the gift of God's Word to the people in your life this Christmas?

PRAY

Father,

It's frightening to think that our words reveal our worth. Rid us of our self-centeredness and make way for the Word within. Let our hearts treasure You and our lips glorify You so that others may be nourished by the gift that will last. Amen.

SATURDAY
Remembered

READ

Luke 1:57-80

PREPARE

Sometimes the beauty, holiness, and mystery of Christmas makes us want to weep or at the very least tear up while no one is watching. It is almost as if the very air is hung with a divine fragrance that isn't there throughout the rest of the year. And I think Zechariah tells us why.

After being unable to speak for nine months, when John was born and Zechariah's silence was lifted, his first words were not, "I have a son!" They were, essentially, "God remembered." In his beautiful prophesy, Zechariah recounted the ways God remembered His promise to Abraham, David, the prophets, and now to Zechariah in the birth of his son who would prepare the way for the coming of the Lord.

When Scripture speaks of God remembering, it always implies much more than just a fleeting thought of a past event. "God's remembering always implies His movement toward [His people],"[31] and Zechariah describes this movement as the feeling of tender mercy falling or the warm sun's rays dawning over people who were perishing in great darkness (Luke 1:78-79). No wonder the air seems hung with mystery, majesty, and beauty at Christmas. Advent reminds us with the coming of Christ, we are remembered and welcomed in as adopted children, inheritors of precious promises, and beloved friends.

Throughout Scripture, God not only tells us He remembers, but He also gives His people the command to remember. In the Old Testament, God commanded His people to remember the event of the Exodus, His act of delivering them from slavery in Egypt. In the New Testament, His people are commanded to remember the death and resurrection of Christ, His act of delivering them from slavery to sin. As God's people obey and remember how He delivered and moved toward them in the past, it helps them anticipate how He will deliver and move toward them again in the present and future.

In his book *The End of Memory*, Miroslav Volf writes, "No matter how hopeless a situation might seem, God will ultimately vindicate the afflicted and judge the wrongdoers involved. Wrongdoing does not have the last word. If we remember a wrongdoing—no matter how horrendous—through the lens of remembering the Exodus, we will remember the wrongdoing as a moment in the history of those who are already on their way to deliverance."[32]

During the Advent season, remembering how God sent John and then Jesus helps our hearts remember we are still a people on our way to deliverance. Jesus came to us once as a baby; He comes to us now through His Spirit; and He will come again as a ruling and reigning King. Wrongdoings, injustices, hardships, and hurts lose their power to have the last word in your life because Jesus does.

So take time this week to remember God's movement toward you through Christ. Enter the mystery of Christmas. It's not just for children; it's for grown adults who, like Zechariah, struggle to believe in a God who remembers, moves toward His people, and always makes good on His promises. Through Immanuel, the tender mercy of our God has risen over our hearts and will one day rise again. "For the Lord God is a sun and shield; the Lord bestows favor and honor. No good thing does he withhold from those who walk uprightly. O Lord of hosts, blessed is the one who trusts in you!" (Psalm 84:11-12). Thank You, O God, for remembering!

CONSIDER

- What is one hard or painful thing you struggle to remember about this past year?

- How can you remember this event through the lens of God's steadfast love and faithfulness (Psalm 26:3), as someone who is on the way to complete deliverance?

- Write out a prayer for someone in your life who needs to remember life through the lens of God's faithful love.

PRAY

Father,

You did not have to remember us. You could have left us as orphans, but You chose to send Your Son so that we could be called children of God (John 1:12). You invite us to remember every difficult memory through the lens of Your steadfast love so that we can be restored and redeemed. Renew our faith, hope, and joy this Christmas season, trusting that because You remembered and came to us once, You will come again. Amen.

ADVENT
WEEK FOUR

THE ANGEL'S CANDLE: LOVE

THE FOURTH SUNDAY OF ADVENT
Hark! the Herald Angels Sing

Before you begin reading, light four candles on your wreath. The fourth candle is the Angel's Candle, which represents love.

READ
Matthew 1:18-25

PREPARE

Most of us have read the angel's message to Joseph so many times that any awe or wonder over the angel's words is long gone. But in a careful reading of the angel's proclamation, the message is as profound today as it was two thousand years ago. Joseph is described as a "just man," unwilling to put Mary through any public scrutiny, shame, or even a possible stoning according to Old Testament law (Leviticus 20:10). Yet the problem remained: his fiancée was pregnant with a baby who was not his.

We are not told if Mary tried to explain to Joseph the angel's message about her baby being the Son of God, or if he struggled to reconcile her words with the reality of her pregnancy. But as he considered, reflected, and pondered, an angel appeared to him.

The angel spoke specifically to Joseph's fears, confirming that this child was not conceived out of sin but from an overshadowing of Mary's womb by the Holy Spirit of God. Matthew expounds on the angel's words and on who this child would be. He is not just any son; He is God's Son, Immanuel—a name meaning "God with us" (Matthew 1:23).

While Joseph's fears about Mary's unfaithfulness were relieved, his fears about his own reputation as a man of integrity and about how to care for this special child and His mother were only beginning. As for Mary, God's favor did not mean easy circumstances for Joseph; it was an invitation to depend on his great God.

Resting in God's favor and obeying the words of the angel meant relying on a wisdom greater than his own. It meant laying aside a safe and secure life and trusting God was in control even when everything appeared to be falling apart. Joseph must have remembered and leaned on the angel's words when the announcement of the census came from Caesar Augustus to travel with his pregnant wife to Bethlehem. He must have leaned on the angel's announcement when the time came for him to flee to Egypt with Mary and Jesus to avoid Herod's murderous wrath (Matthew 2:13-15).

Sometimes the most loving and courageous thing we can do for the people in our care is to risk our safe plans and secure future by entrusting ourselves to a God who calls us to radical obedience and absolute dependence on Him. We are not told exactly how the details of our story will play out, but we are promised Immanuel will be with us. That is what gives us the confidence to step out and obey.

As Christmas Day draws close and the year comes to an end, is there a decision you are wrestling with? A step of obedience God is calling you to take but you want to resist? If so, take heart. Whatever God calls you to do won't come with all the details or a ten-year plan. But it will come with the courage to take the next step as you rely on the promise that God will not only equip you but be with you every step of the way.

CONSIDER

- Are there any unexpected or surprising circumstances in your life right now that make you feel uncertain about your future? Explain.

- Where do you sense God calling you to take the next step of obedience and trust Him in new and courageous ways? If so, what does that next step look like?

- Write out a prayer casting your cares on the Lord. Be honest about your fears and ask Him to remind you He will be with you every step of the way, no matter what He calls you to do.

ADVENT ACTIVITIES

Choose one of the following activities this week to help you remember the love Immanuel brings during this season.

- **Announce the good news.** Purchase a set of Christmas cards and stamps. Prayerfully consider who might need the reminder that God is with them in this season. Act as messengers of hope, writing those people a note of encouragement, pointing them to the hope found in Jesus, our Immanuel. This can be a good activity to do with a group of friends or as a family, even if you have older kids or teens.

If you have younger kids, consider making a craft angel with an encouraging message. Decorate a brown paper bag as an angel puppet. Help kids write out "Jesus came to save us, and He is always with us" on the back side of the puppet. When people come to visit, invite your kids to use the puppet to share their special message with your family or friends.

- **Share a message of love.** Use a globe, atlas, or online map to pick a country. Pray each night for the people in this country who don't know about Jesus, asking God to send His messengers to take the good news of Christmas to people who are waiting to hear.

PRAY

Father,

The life You call us to isn't always safe or easy, but Your plans are always good. Give my heart the courage to trust You even when I cannot clearly see the way. Remind me that Your presence and steadfast love will be with me throughout every step of the journey. May my life and my plans reflect the confidence and security I find in following You. Amen.

CLOSING CAROL:
"HARK! THE HERALD ANGELS SING"

Hark! the herald angels sing,
"Glory to the newborn King:
peace on earth, and mercy mild,
God and sinners reconciled!"
Joyful, all ye nations, rise,
join the triumph of the skies;
with th'angelic hosts proclaim,
"Christ is born in Bethlehem!"

Hark! the herald angels sing,
"Glory to the newborn King"

Christ, by highest heaven adored,
Christ, the everlasting Lord,
late in time behold him come,
offspring of the Virgin's womb:
veiled in flesh the Godhead see;
hail th'incarnate Deity,
pleased with us in flesh to dwell,
Jesus, our Immanuel.

Hark! the herald angels sing,
"Glory to the newborn King"

Hail the heaven-born Prince of Peace!
Hail the Sun of Righteousness!
Light and life to all he brings,
risen with healing in his wings.
Mild he lays his glory by,
born that we no more may die,
born to raise us from the earth,
born to give us second birth.

Hark! the herald angels sing,
"Glory to the newborn King"

MONDAY
The Journey

READ
Matthew 2:1-15

PREPARE
Yesterday began the fourth Sunday of Advent, which means we only have one week before Christmas. One more week until the last Christmas party has been attended, the last carol has been sung, and the last present has been unwrapped. But with all the hustle and bustle ahead, don't forget to prepare the way for your heart to fully celebrate the day of Christ's birth.

Throughout Scripture, angels are heralds, protectors, warriors, defenders, and worshipers of God. Angels played an important role in the birth of Christ, just as they did throughout the Old Testament. In the Christmas story, the angels announced the coming of Jesus, the Son of God, our Savior, our Immanuel. Joseph almost divorced Mary; Herod almost killed Jesus; and Zechariah almost didn't believe. But in each instance, an angel of the Lord intervened, declaring God's plan and reminding His people to trust in Him. We continue to declare their same message today: Jesus came to save His people from their sins (Matthew 1:21), and His kingdom will have no end (Luke 1:33).

Sometimes this message comes to us suddenly, and they are given extraordinary faith to believe like Mary. But sometimes our journey of faith is more gradual like the journey of the wise men. From the time the star appeared in the east to the time it came to rest over the place where Jesus was in Bethlehem is thought to be anywhere from a few months to a few years.

While everyone's story of how they ended up in loving relationship with Jesus is different, one thing remains constant and clear: "The longing for nearness to God will not be fulfilled in a stroke. Anyone who wants God must also go on a journey."[33] It might be a long journey of laying aside fears about having a safe and secure future like Joseph. It might be a journey of laying aside the defense of your good name and reputation for a time like Mary. It might be a journey of learning to trust that God can do the impossible like Zechariah. Or it might be a journey of plucking up roots from your comforts and culture and even changing locations like the wise men.

Whatever your story, whatever you have to lay aside, the goal is the same: worship. We are to bring all that we are and offer all that we have at His feet. When we do, whatever we leave at the altar pales in comparison to what we gain.

What hinders your worship this Christmas season? What comforts do you find difficult to let go of? What gifts of your time, expertise, and finances are you reluctant to give? This last week of Advent, and throughout the remainder of the year, go on a journey with God. Be willing to step out in obedience to travel with Him, no matter the distance. Thanks to the extravagant love of God, the way is open, the road is clear, and the goal is certain. Once you arrive to give Christ your gifts, the fullness of your heart will far outweigh any emptiness in your hands.

CONSIDER

- Trace the steps of your journey with Jesus. How did you end up in loving relationship with Him?

- What hindrances keep you from wanting to continue in your journey with God?

- What gifts of your time, finances, or expertise are you being led to give to Christ this Christmas season?

PRAY

Father,

Thank You for going to great lengths to give us Your Son. We know His journey was not easy and that access to Your presence was bought with a great price. May we listen to whatever You have to say this Advent season and go on a journey to give You our worship wherever You lead. Amen.

TUESDAY
How We Wait

READ

Luke 2:22-38

PREPARE

For young children, waiting for Christmas Day can seem like an eternity. For those of us who are older and wiser, waiting for the holidays seems like a walk in the park compared to some of the other things we are waiting on. We are all waiting for something, but when we are waiting for a spouse to change, a job to materialize, a baby to arrive, or a broken heart to mend, this is when waiting becomes difficult. This is in part because deep down we never really know if we will ever actually get what we are waiting for.

Waiting can be a painful exercise of learning to trust God, no matter what the outcome of our wait eventually is. What if we never marry? What if we are always barren? What if the job we always wanted or the move we always dreamed of never happens? What if life is just one long bated breath or one big disappointment waiting to happen? This space is where we live most of our lives, not in the excitement of our hopes being realized but in the in-between times as we wait.

The rest of this week, while we continue to wait for Christmas Day to arrive, I want to talk about how we wait beyond the Advent season in the everyday moments of life. What exactly does waiting look like in the remaining eleven months of the year? To help us answer that question, it's helpful to look at the lives of Simeon and Anna.

Both Simeon and Anna knew what it meant to wait. Luke tells us they were both advanced in age and had spent many years hoping, praying, and waiting for the redemption of God's people to appear. When Joseph, Mary, and Jesus arrived at the temple, Anna was eighty-four years old.

Luke also tells us that Anna "did not depart from the temple, worshiping with fasting and prayer night and day" and that Simeon was "righteous and devout" as they waited for the Messiah to appear (Luke 2:25, 37). They didn't sit on their hands and allow bitterness or cynicism to creep in, dulling their desire for God or deadening their worship. Instead of isolating themselves in unanswered questions, they actively waited on God through the disciplines of worship and righteous living.

We can learn to wait like Anna and Simeon and take seriously the Word of God that defines waiting as "to bind together (perhaps by twisting)."[34] Rather than becoming a place of stagnation and despair, waiting can become a place of movement and intimacy with God as we choose to bind our souls to Him. This is where our questions become less of an issue, and we stop fearing we will never get what we are waiting for. Our waiting becomes more about knowing God and being known than about getting what we want.

When we wait with God, we always get what we are waiting for, because our soul's desire ends up being God Himself (Psalm 16:11; 62:1). And like Anna and Simeon, one day we will see the fruit of our wait: we will see Jesus face to face and never stop giving thanks, not only for our Immanuel but also for how our wait increased our longing for Him.

CONSIDER

- When have you waited on something so long that you felt your heart growing cold or hard toward God?

- What spiritual practices help keep your heart soft toward God and satisfied in Him as you wait?

- Write out a prayer asking God to help you remember that what you are waiting for can only be found in practicing the presence of God and binding your heart to His, no matter how long you wait.

PRAY

Father,

Waiting is so hard, and sometimes we question whether we wait in vain for the things we want the most. But we believe, no matter how long or how hard our wait is, all our desires will one day be met in You. In the meantime, keep us close to You as we wait through corporate worship, the reading of Your Word, prayer, fasting, and giving thanks. As we do so, we will find our hearts continually satisfied in You. Amen.

WEDNESDAY
The Hidden Years

READ

Luke 2:39-52

PREPARE

We know very little about the years of Jesus's life in-between His encounter with Anna and Simeon in the temple and the inauguration of His ministry through His baptism by the Jordan River. In fact, we know the details of just one event. At twelve years of age, Jesus accompanied His parents in their journey to Jerusalem for the Passover Feast. When it was time to return home to Nazareth, Mary and Joseph assumed Jesus was in the group of relatives and friends returning with them. Only after a day's journey did they realize Jesus wasn't with them. They returned to Jerusalem and searched for Him for three days.

While they might not have fully understood who Jesus was, they knew He was a special kid. They knew His birth was heralded by angels and a powerful king had wanted Him murdered. One can only assume fearful thoughts ran through their minds as they looked for Him. But all along, Jesus was where, quite frankly, Mary and Joseph should have known He would be: His Father's house.

Jesus returned with them to Nazareth and "was submissive to them" (Luke 2:51). This is nothing short of phenomenal considering that twelve-year-old Jesus had just spent several days in the temple with the wisest teachers in Israel hanging on His every word. But Jesus submitted and obeyed, not just for His return trip home but for the next eighteen years. The author of Hebrews confirms this when he writes, "Although he was a son, he learned obedience through what he suffered. And being made perfect, he became the source of eternal salvation to all who obey him" (Hebrews 5:8-9). Jesus's suffering included more than the cross; it also included learning to submit to and honor imperfect parents.

Jesus's preparation for His three years of ministry were in His thirty years of anonymity. God did not need a Son who was wise in His own eyes; He needed a Son willing to humbly obey, even when He understood more than His parents or other authority figures. Alicia Britt Chole writes, "Though unpopular, these hidden places are not unproductive; within them God houses the unglamorous guts of a truly fruitful existence."[35] We want a life made up of majestic moments, but most of life is lived in the mundane. But in those moments, as we wait on God's timing to step out in obedience, God is shaping us into people who can His will.

During the Advent season, as we remember that Christ came and wait for Him to come again, we must also remember that most of our lives will be made up of moments in hidden years. Most of our days will not be lived out on a platform before people hanging on our every word. Our lives will be forged in the fires of everyday obedience. This doesn't happen overnight. Like Jesus, we are shaped into submissive, obedient people as we suffer and obey when no one else is watching. And like Jesus, as we wait, submit, and obey every day, we will flourish. We too will increase in "wisdom and in stature and in favor with God and man" (Luke 2:52), ready for the call that can be carried out only through lessons learned in hiddenness.

CONSIDER

- In what area(s) of your life do you feel your obedience to God seems unseen or hidden?

- How does knowing God used Jesus's hidden years to prepare Him for His years of effective ministry encourage your heart?

- How can you encourage someone today who feels hidden or unseen, letting them know you see their submission to God and their love for others?

PRAY

Father,

Forgive me for resisting submission to You and insisting instead on my own way. This Advent season, remind me that as You formed Jesus's character in the furnace of waiting and suffering, You will form mine as well. The hidden places of my life are where You do Your greatest work. May I increase in wisdom as I wait, just as Jesus did. Amen.

THURSDAY
Our Conquering King

READ

Luke 23:26-49; Revelation 19:6-21

PREPARE

It might seem strange to include an account of the crucifixion of Christ in a collection of Advent readings, but as we anticipate the coming of Christ on Christmas, we also anticipate the day He will come again. But while He came the first time to die, He will come again to rule and to reign. As Cyril of Jerusalem wrote in the fourth century AD, "We preach not one advent only of Christ, but a second also, far more glorious than the former. For the former gave a view of His patience; but the latter brings with it the crown of a divine kingdom."[36]

Throughout His trial and crucifixion, even Christ Himself anticipated His second coming. On the road to Calvary, He turned to the mourners and lamenters following Him, saying, "Do not weep for me, but weep for yourselves and for your children" (Luke 23:28). Jesus could see a day coming that no one else could see—a day of destruction of the temple in Jerusalem but also the day He would return to end the enemies of God.

Jesus's vision and mindset through His suffering gives us the key for how we are to wait and endure through our times of suffering. If all we can see is the suffering in front of us, we will surely give up. But if we lift our eyes from our circumstances and set our gaze on the King who came and is coming again, we too will have the strength to endure. Like Christ, we must remember that whatever cross we are given to bear is temporary but the glory that awaits us is eternal (2 Corinthians 4:17-18).

Revelation 19 gives us a picture of this glory. When Christ returns the second time, He is not coming back as the meek and lowly sacrificial Lamb; He is returning as the conquering King, a rider on a white horse whose name is Faithful and True. He will judge and make war against the enemies of God and rule the nations with a rod of iron. The opportunity to willingly submit to the crucified Christ will have ended; on the day He returns, every knee must bow to the King of the Kings and the Lord of Lords (Philippians 2:9-11).

This Advent season, as we wait for Jesus, we wait while walking the road of the cross. To each of His followers, Jesus says, "Take up [your] cross and follow me" (Matthew 16:24-25). But like Jesus on the road to Calvary, we have a choice. We can focus on our suffering, allowing it to consume us, or we can look to Jesus, "the founder and perfecter of our faith" (Hebrews 12:2). He has not left us alone in our suffering; He always comes for us as Immanuel. His Spirit is with us in our suffering, comforting and encouraging us every step of the way.

Christmas Day will bring with it so much joy as we remember the Child who came. But it pales in comparison to the joy we will experience when our King comes again. He is preparing a place for us far beyond our wildest imaginings (John 14:2-3), and we will celebrate our homecoming at the marriage supper of the Lamb (Revelation 19:9). Every wound will be healed, every wrong will be made right, every tear will be wiped away, and every sorrow will be redeemed.

CONSIDER

- Read the description of Christ once again in Revelation 19:11-16. How does knowing how Christ will return change your view of your present suffering?

- Now read 2 Corinthians 4:16-18. What "unseen" things can you fix your eyes on today to help you endure any affliction you are facing?

- Take a moment to thank Jesus for coming once as a helpless baby and ask that you would have a heart ready for His return as a conquering King.

PRAY

Father,

We have yet to see Christ return to make all wrongs right, so we wait. In the busyness of the next few days, may we be quiet enough to hear the invitation to the marriage supper of the Lamb. Remind us this Advent not only of the stable but also of the King who is coming. Keep us waiting, watching, and alert, ready for His arrival. Amen.

FRIDAY
The Healing Shepherd

READ

1 Peter 2:18-25; Revelation 7:9-17

PREPARE

Learning how to forgive is part and parcel of our daily bread as believers in Christ. In the prayer He taught us how to pray, Jesus puts the both the need to be forgiven and the need to forgive within the context of asking for our daily bread: "Give us this day our daily bread, and forgive us our debts, as we also have forgiven our debtors" (Matthew 6:11-12). Forgiving others for their very real sin, hurts, and slights against us is not a one-time event or infrequent occurrence; it is a discipline we must do daily.[37]

Forgiving those who treat us unjustly is not a suggestion; it is a calling on our lives as believers in Christ (1 Peter 2:21). In this passage, Peter does not just tell us we are called to forgive; he shows us how we are equipped to forgive. When unfair or unjust treatment occurs, we walk through it with our minds "full" of God (1 Peter 2:19). Our thoughts do not repeatedly replay the offense that has been committed against us, nor do we rehearse justified words of reproach condemning our enemies' actions. Far from it. We are to turn our thoughts to God. We remember that at the height of the unfair treatment He experienced from others, Jesus didn't sin, get even, or threaten people. So, instead of harsh, angry words and vengeful speeches, we rehearse and repeat in our heads the silence of the One who suffered on our behalf.

We remember that we are not just the victims; we too are perpetrators. It was our sin that held Jesus on the cross. It was our unjust treatment of the only righteous One that condemned Him to an unfair death in our place. Once we realize we are ever and always the sinner as well as the sinned against, we can let our offenses go, entrusting them to the only One who ever truly suffered blamelessly and unjustly.

And by *His* wounds, we are healed. We are healed of our need to always give a retort. We are healed of our need to justify our actions or character. We are free to leave our life and reputation, our past, present, and future in the hands of Him who judges justly. We are free to eat the fruit of right relationship with God and others because Christ ate the bitter fruit of the cross for us.

As much as we must be mindful of the example Christ set for us and our need to forgive those who sin against us, we must also be mindful of our future. This future is the picture that Revelation 7 so beautifully paints. We are free to let go of our need to protect and defend ourselves because we are headed to a place where God's presence provides for us forever. Because our Shepherd became the sacrificial Lamb, our tears will be wiped away and transformed into joy. Any wrongs perpetrated against us will be made right.

As Advent draws to a close and we draw closer to Christmas Day, know that your freedom to forgive is one of the greatest gifts you have been given. You are free to release the grudges you hold and the wounds you have to the Shepherd and Overseer of your soul. As you do so, you will find rest, restoration, and the fruit of righteousness now and forever.

CONSIDER

- What hurts and grudges are you carrying into the Christmas season this year? What would it take for you to release them into Jesus's capable hands?

- How does being mindful of God while enduring unfair treatment help you quietly entrust yourself to Him who judges justly?

- Close today by writing out a prayer asking God as your Shepherd to help you let go of any unforgiveness you hold so that you can be healed.

PRAY

Father,

We find ourselves rehashing wrongs done to us and rehearsing speeches of anger more often than we would like to admit. Please forgive us. Instead of being mindful of our grudges, help us to be mindful of Christ. When He was treated unfairly, "he did not threaten, but continued entrusting himself to him who judges justly" (1 Peter 2:23). Equip us to follow His example, remembering our own sin as much as we remember the sin of others. As we entrust our lives into Your hands, may our wounds be healed. Amen.

SATURDAY
Coming Home

READ

Luke 12:35-40; Revelation 22:1-7

PREPARE

Christmas day arrives tomorrow. No matter how wonderful or difficult the celebrations are tomorrow, no matter how they fill our hearts or leave us with an empty ache, for all who love Jesus and long His return, one thing is true: we are not home yet. We have glimpses of our forever home in Christmas Eve candlelight services, in the reading of the Word, and in the singing of hope-filled songs like "Silent Night." But once the service is over, the last meal is served, and the last gift is unwrapped, many of us feel sad that Christmas is finished and we must wait in the everyday once again.

But the reading today gives our aching hearts hope. It gives us confidence that because Jesus really did come as a baby—swaddled in humanity, helplessness, and poverty—He really will come again in glory.

This is what the parable in Luke 12 is all about. The word used for "dressed" in verse 37 comes from the same word used in John 13 the night before Jesus died: "Jesus, knowing that the Father had given all things into his hands, and that he had come from God and was going back to God, rose from supper. He laid aside his outer garments, and taking a towel, *tied* it around his waist" (John 13:3-4, emphasis added).[38]

Jesus's confidence to gird Himself with a towel and

take on a servant's job came from His knowledge of who He was and where He was headed. He knew this earth was not His home; it was a place to live out His call to obey His Father and to love His people back to life. The same is true for us. Our confidence to live in the everyday after the holy day comes from knowing who we are and where we are headed. Home with Christ is not a myth or fantasy; it is as real as the manger in Bethlehem. So today, we anticipate the joy of Christmas, but even more, we anticipate the joy of going home.

As we read about yesterday in 1 Peter 2, while we wait out our days here on this earth, asking for forgiveness and forgiving others is part and parcel of our daily bread. We will always be mindful of the tree of death (the cross) Christ climbed for us so that we might eat the tree of life. This is the reminder that Revelation 22 gives. Healing is coming. Full redemption of sorrows is on its way. Feasting, merriment, celebration, awe, worship, and joy will be ours without end once we are home seated at the table of King Jesus.

Until then, we wait. But we do not wait as without hope (1 Thessalonians 4:13). We wait while remembering God moved toward us once as Immanuel in the form of Jesus, and He moves toward us again every day in the presence of His Spirit in our hearts. We keep hope alive and the light burning as we read the hopeful words of the prophets, the peaceful promises of the King from Bethlehem, the joyful news of the shepherds, and the loving announcements of the angels. The way is open, the King has come, and the King will come again. Let Love gird His waist and serve you today as you unwrap the gift of His birth while feasting on His promise to come again.

CONSIDER

- What parts of the preparations for Christmas this year have brought your heart joy? What parts have left your heart a bit empty?

- What aspects of your forever home are you looking forward to the most?

- How does remembering who you are and where you are headed encourage your heart on Christmas Eve?

PRAY

Father,

Our hearts are full of hope and wonder that You came as a baby two thousand years ago to make Your home with us. But as wonderful as our Christmas celebrations are, we are still left with an ache and the hope that You will come again. Prepare our hearts to celebrate Your birth tomorrow and prepare us to walk the way of the coming King throughout the rest of the year. May the way we remember the words of the prophets, walk the road to Bethlehem, run with joy like the shepherds, and receive Your love in the announcement of the angels prepare our hearts for our forever home with You. Amen.

CHRISTMAS DAY
The Way of the King

Before you begin reading, light four candles on your wreath, along with the Christ Candle in the center, which represents the birth of Christ.

READ
Isaiah 40:1-5; Luke 2:1-21

PREPARE
Several years ago, our family traveled to the city of Rome. We toured ancient ruins, viewed masterpieces, and ate mounds of gelato when our feet were too tired to walk anymore. Rome is both beautiful and impressive by any measure, but many buildings that were once considered to be centers of power and influence now lie in ruins. During our tour of the Forum, the heart of city life in ancient Rome, our guide pointed out the Curia Julia building where the Roman Senate met, making laws for the Roman people and issuing decrees. From this building, it was likely that Caesar Augustus issued the decree that "all the world should be registered" (Luke 2:1), setting into motion the fulfillment of prophecy that a king would be born in Bethlehem who would both save and rule the world.

When Caesar decreed his census, it is likely he had never heard of the town of Bethlehem. The entire Roman province of

Judea was relatively inconsequential in relation to the rest of his empire. But two thousand years later, Caesar Augustus's Forum is a heap of ruins. While students today still read about him in history books, his name no longer holds any power nor his government any earthly sway. When Caesar died, his rule and reign died with him.

But this baby born in Bethlehem to young, impoverished parents without money or ability to even secure a room in an inn for his arrival has an unshakeable kingdom that knows no end. He rules and reigns in the hearts of all He came to serve and lays low the mightiest person through His enduring power, strength, forgiveness, and love.

This is the way of our King. The birth of Christ reminds us that God's ways are not our ways. As we have seen the last four weeks of Advent, the path to true leadership is service. The call to enduring greatness is humility. The way to preserve your life is to lose it in Him. The way to wait, hope, and endure through suffering is by entrusting your heart to the One who suffered for you and whose love never fails. It is to this Savior that we come today—insignificant in the eyes of the world but enduring in the hearts of those who still worship at His manger.

Today, in the early morning hours, seated around the table with people you love, or late in the evening when the festivities have quieted down, enjoy Jesus. Adore your Wonderful Counselor, Mighty God, Everlasting Father, and Prince of Peace (Isaiah 9:6). And today, if your past feels like a heap of ruins, if your present feels empty, if your future looks bleak, take heart. Consider Caesar, and then consider Jesus. Our greatest comfort comes from a Savior who set aside temporary power, came humbly as a man, died on a cross, rose from the ruins, and gives us everlasting life. Today, while our wait for celebrating His birth is over, we continue to wait in hope and healing for His return. Merry Christmas!

CONSIDER

- What is your favorite part of the Christmas story in Luke 2? What about the birth of Jesus stirs your heart to worship Him today?

- Picture the ruins of Caesar's Forum, and then consider the humble manger of Jesus. How does considering both of those things encourage and strengthen your heart today?

- Ask God to give you a heart that continues to prepare the way for the coming King in the days beyond the Christmas season.

CHRISTMAS DAY ACTIVITIES

Choose one of the following activities today to help you savor the joy of Christmas more fully.

- As a family, read the Christmas story in Luke 2:1-21. Let each family member share what his/her favorite part of the story is.

- Spend some time in prayer with your friends or family— whomever you've been celebrating Advent with—thanking the Father for the gift of Jesus and that His true home is in the hearts of those who love Him and call Him Savior and Lord.

PRAY

Father,

Having a humble heart is an essential part of celebrating Christmas and continuing to prepare the way for Jesus. Forgive me for valuing worldly influence, power, and wealth above the gentle, humble heart of my King (Matthew 11:29). Help me remember anything I build for my own name will perish, but when I lose my life to serve Your Name, then, and only then, will I rise to everlasting life. Thank You for coming and for Your promise to come again. Keep my heart ready for Your return all year long. Amen.

CLOSING CAROL:
"O COME, ALL YE FAITHFUL"

O come, all ye faithful, joyful and triumphant,
O come ye, O come ye to Bethlehem!
Come and behold Him, born the King of angels!

O come, let us adore Him,
O come, let us adore Him,
O come, let us adore Him, Christ the Lord.

Sing choirs of angels; sing in exultation;
sing, all ye citizens of heaven above!
Glory to God, glory in the highest!

O come, let us adore Him,
O come, let us adore Him,
O come, let us adore Him, Christ the Lord.

Yea, Lord, we greet Thee, born this happy morning;
Jesus, to Thee be all glory giv'n!
Word of the Father, now in flesh appearing!
O come, let us adore Him,
O come, let us adore Him,
O come, let us adore Him, Christ the Lord.

NOTES

[1] "What Is the Meaning of the Advent Season?," University of Portland, accessed September 25, 2024, https://www.up.edu/garaventa/did-you-know/meaning-advent.html#:~:text=The%20word%20%E2%80%9CAdvent%E2%80%9D%20is%20derived,of%20the%20Greek%20word%20parousia.

[2] Jonathon Gibson, O Come, O Come Emmanuel: A Liturgy for Daily Worship from Advent to Epiphany (Wheaton, Illinois: Crossway, 2023), 31.

[3] Bruce K. Waltke, The Book of Proverbs: Chapters 1–15 (Grand Rapids, Michigan: William B. Eerdmans Publishing Company, 2004), 245.

[4] J.R.R. Tolkien, The Lord of the Rings (New York: Houghton Mifflin Company, 1994), 847.

[5] Dietrich Bonhoeffer, God is in the Manger: Reflections on Advent and Christmas (Louisville, Kentucky: Westminster John Knox Press, 2010), 5.

[6] F.B. Meyer, Love to the Uttermost (Charleston, South Carolina: BiblioBazaar, 2007), 20.

[7] "Q & A 42," in Heidelberg Catechism, accessed September 12, 2024, https://www.crcna.org/welcome/beliefs/confessions/heidelberg-catechism.

[8] Augustine, quoted by Jonathon Gibson in O Come, O Come Emmanuel: A Liturgy for Daily Worship from Advent to Epiphany (Wheaton, Illinois: Crossway, 2023), 71.

[9] Michael Reeves, Rejoice and Tremble: The Surprising Good News of the Fear of the Lord (Wheaton, Illinois: Crossway, 2021), 43.

[10] Warren Patrick Baker, ed., Hebrew-Greek Key Word Study Bible: English Standard Version (Chattanooga, TN: AMG Publishers, 2013), 1641.

[11] Baker, 1907.

[12] Derek Kidner, Psalms 1-72 (Downers Grove, IL: InterVarsity Press, 2008), 208.

[13] Tremper Longman III, Psalms: An Introduction and Commentary (Downers Grove, IL: InterVarsity Press, 2014), 35.

[14] Longman, 35.

[15] Alec Motyer, Psalms by the Day: A New Devotional Translation (Scotland, UK: Christian Focus Publications, 2016), 14.

[16] Kidner, Psalms 1-72, 66.

[17] Baker, Hebrew-Greek Key Word Study Bible: English Standard Version, #5547, 2327.

[18] Timothy Keller, The Songs of Jesus: A Year of Daily Devotions in the Psalms (New York: Viking, 2015), 3.

[19] Kidner, 69.

[20] Kidner, 70.

[21] J. Alec Motyer, Isaiah: An Introduction and Commentary (Downers Grove, IL: IVP Academic, 1999), 76.

[22] Motyer, 116.

[23] Dietrich Bonhoeffer, God is in the Manger: Reflections on Advent and Christmas (Louisville, Kentucky: Westminster John Knox Press, 2010), 13.

[24] Motyer, Isaiah, 117.

[25] Motyer, 117.

[26] Motyer, 121.

[27] Motyer, 122.

[28] John Newton, "Dependence on Christ-God's Prescriptions," The Reformed Reader, August 19, 1775, https://www.reformedreader.org/rbb/newton/letter04.htm.

[29] Newton, "Dependence on Christ-God's Prescriptions"

[30] Timothy Keller, The Songs of Jesus: A Year of Daily Devotions in the Psalms (New York: Viking, 2015), viii.

[31] Kidner, 84.

[32] Miroslav Volf, The End of Memory: Remembering Rightly in a Violent World (Grand Rapids, Michigan: William B. Eerdmans Publishing Company, 2006), 108-109.

[33] Keller, 206.

[34] Warren Patrick Baker, ed., Hebrew-Greek Key Word Study Bible: English Standard Version (Chattanooga, TN: AMG Publishers, 2013), #6960, 1906.

[35] Alicia Britt Chole, Anonymous (Nashville, TN: Thomas Nelson, 2006) 60.

[36] Cyril of Jerusalem, quoted by Jonathon Gibson, O Come, O Come Emmanuel: A Liturgy for Daily Worship from Advent to Epiphany (Wheaton, Illinois: Crossway, 2023), 41.

[37] "What Forgiveness Is and Isn't (The Lord's Prayer Pt. 4), BibleProject Podcast, Sermon om the Mount, episode 23, June 3, 2024, https://bibleproject.com/podcast/what-forgiveness-and-isnt-lords-prayer-pt-4/.

[38] Warren Patrick Baker, ed., Hebrew-Greek Key Word Study Bible: English Standard Version (Chattanooga, TN: AMG Publishers, 2013), #1241, #2224, #4024, 2080, 2143, 2240.

ABOUT THE AUTHOR
Susannah Baker

SUSANNAH BAKER is an author, Bible study teacher, and founder of Restore retreats for women. She is the author of the book and companion Bible study *Restore: Remembering Life's Hurts with the God Who Rebuilds*. She has written several other studies, including her newest one *Rebuild: Connecting to God Through the Psalms*, a prayer guide, and numerous free tools for people to use in their own journey of healing and hope with Christ. Through her resources, she loves to help people rebuild and restore secure connection to God through His Word, prayer, and relationship to Jesus Christ.

Susannah has her degree from Texas A&M University and lives in Houston, Texas. Apart from Jesus Christ, her greatest loves are her husband, Jason, and her four beautiful daughters. Her favorite Christmas carol is *O Come, O Come, Emmanuel*, and her favorite Christmas tradition is celebrating Advent each Sunday around the dinner table with her family.

For more information about Susannah, visit **www.susannahbaker.com**.

JOY IN THE JOURNEY

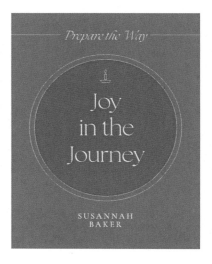

For the season of Advent, I invite you to download the Scripture reading guide that corresponds with the devotions in this book. It's a helpful reminder to place in your Bible, on your kitchen counter or in your workspace to prepare the way for the coming King.

www.susannahbaker.com/resources